Twisted

This book and the building are dedicated to the memory of Shun Yen Siu (1940-2013), CEO of Lafayette 148 New York, 1996-2013, without whose vision they would not have been possible.

Twisted

Acknowledgements

A project of this scale and complexity, conducted across the globe, has, undoubtedly, involved many. There is however, always a driving force that sets the trajectory of a project like this one. In this case, that force was Lafayette 148 New York, with Mr. Siu at its helm. Without his un-wavering support, and insistence, this project would not have happened. For that, we are grateful.

The work at our Buffalo office was undertaken by Christopher Romano, Adesh Michael Singh, Michael O'Hara, Jose Chang, Maciej Kaczynski, and Dave Nardozzi.

Matthew La Monte assisted in collating the material, corresponding texts and images, and working on the packaging of the book. Julia Brooks assisted in preparing models and drawings for photography by Cody Goddard.

The production of this book was made possible with support from the Stuckeman School, Pennsylvania State University, through the Chair of Integrative Design, the University of Michigan's Taubman College Office of Research, and Lafayette 148.

We want to acknowledge the tireless and brilliant team at Lafayette 148 New York who worked closely with us throughout. They are Ida Siu, Harvey and Jenny Lok, and Lily Chen. The driving force of the company includes President, Deirdre Quinn and Creative Director, Barbara Gast. In Shantou Anita Wong, Larry Wong, and Jonathan Chan were invaluable. Thank you to this amazing team.

The full documentation of the L-148 building was done by the Shanghai-based photographer But Sou Lai. His remarkable craft highlighted our work in the most precise way.

Our counterparts in China, Shantou City Construction Consortium, served as the architects of record. And finally, we acknowledge the labor of hundreds of caring individuals that worked with dedication to create the building that is the subject of this book.

L-148

Marc J Neveu

Completed in 2008 by Mehrdad Hadighi of Studio for Architecture and Tsz Yan Ng, L-148 houses all of the functions of the Lafayette 148 clothing label. The building is organized around the flow of production, literally from conception to shipment of the final product. Office and design studios are placed at the top. Each stage of production is stacked on the floors below. The entry level functions as showroom and has the ability to transform into a runway. The building is, however, much more than a diagram of production. Throughout the building the architects deftly carved into the block to allow light to penetrate into the core and even provide exterior spaces that one is able to occupy. These spaces also help to mitigate the use of artificial cooling by drawing hot air from the building. Post-tensioned beams span the entire width of the floors, thus removing any need for interior columns. The result is a truly free plan that accommodates the wide variety of programmatic needs as well as offering bright and open workspaces.

Three sides of the building are wrapped by a fabric-like double-façade. Composed of a series of free flowing concrete fins, the façade flirts with the viewer offering a peek, here and there. At night it becomes even more revealing. The design of the façade claims a relationship back to the local tradition of concrete construction. In Shantou, the architects found themselves in a situation in which concrete construction was the norm (though often concealed) and on-site poured in-place concrete production was not prohibitively expensive but actually more efficient. The architects designed re-usable formwork from which a family of concrete fins is produced. The fins are hung at various angles, flowing into one another, to produce an array of effects. The effects are, however, not simply visual. The façade operates as a shading device and masks operable windows. The combination of shading and airflow though the building has resulted in a cost savings of forty percent in energy consumption relative to similar manufacturing buildings in the region. Air conditioning is used infrequently and only to reduce humidity. The play of the façade also relates to the performance of the program within.

Each fin was produced on site and with local labor. Holes were punched out of the concrete fins and perform in a number of fascinating ways. The holes lighten the twisted fins to be more easily hung. During the construction process, chain pulleys looped through the holes and allowed for the fins to be picked up, transported and finally set in place. The holes also provide for a play of shadow on the interior surfaces. Contrary to the all too typical scenario that finds large western companies exploiting the inexpensive, and often unethical, labor practices in China, at L-148 the architects are dependent upon and also develop the local tradition.

Similar to the design process, the organization of the book is intentionally non-linear. The five topics – mass-crafting, carving, sculpting, glazing, and modulating – all verbs, contain descriptions of the building process. Interwoven are a series of essays that present distinct but interrelated responses to the many questions that arise when building a garment factory facility in contemporary China. Issues addressed range from the architectural import of the building typology, to the ecological footprint of a factory, to social concerns regarding labor as well as construction practices, to the ethics and aesthetics of factory building. Clear tensions exist between the global and the local, with respect to issues such as material economies, labor relations, working conditions, and company branding. In all of this, what is the role of design? For what can the architect be held responsible in contemporary praxis? Is it ultimately possible to address the social inequalities produced by global garment manufacturing through design? This book is not intended as a monograph but will include extensive documentation of the design process, the development of working drawings, as well as images of the completed building.

Mass-Crafting

Mehrdad Hadighi

"The ground-level plane of the Gothic Journeyman is opposed to the metric plane of the architect, which is on paper and off site. The plane of consistency or composition is opposed to another plane, that of organization or formation. Stone cutting by squaring is opposed to stone cutting using templates, which implies the erection of a model for reproduction."[1]

When Gilles Deleuze, and Félix Guattari wrote the above statement in 1980, the electronic revolution and the internet had not quite reached the level of ubiquity we experience today. Their statement forecasted a future based on a trajectory that was already charted from the pre-industrial world to the first industrial revolution and the rise of machines of the late eighteenth century, to the birth of mass production through the invention of electricity in late nineteenth century, and the development of electronics in the late twentieth century. The work of the architect, in this trajectory, has gone from the work of the Gothic journeyman, cutting stones by squaring, to the contemporary architect, downloading construction details from the manufacturer's website for pre-designed building assemblies and forwarding templates for CNC mills to cut stone to shape.

The journeyman's logic of operation could not exist outside of the territory of the stone, outside of its material configurations and particularities. The journeyman's pitch, punch, claw, chisel, ax, compass, dividers, and set-squares were a reflection of the logic and formation of the stone itself. In application, the journeyman had to materially participate in the territory in question. He had to physically engage the stone, its surfaces, its material inconsistencies, and its nuances. The stone-cutting techniques had to also be continuously altered according to the terrain of the stone. On the other hand, the template, though far more precise in its measure, neutralizes the territory and the participants. The same template will cut Carrara marble as it would Pennsylvania blue stone.

This is not introduced to suggest nostalgia for a manual, mechanical, or analog world. On the contrary, in our work, we are in search of a material tactility and a material language with real-time engagement and real-material consequences in a mediated, binary environment of computer-numerically-controlled mass-production. We are in search of a productive model that is on paper and off-site, which is mediated and computational, that engages mass-production industries, with on-site material sensibilities and labor considerations. We are in search of a productive model that is mediated, yet material, which may be mass-produced with the measured precision of the CNC mill,

1. Gilles Deleuze, and Félix Guattari, *A Thousand Plateaus*, (University of Minnesota Press, Minneapolis, Minnesota, 1987): 368.

and can yet experience the journeyman's craft of squaring. This model is neither solely about organization, nor composition. It is an organization that has entered the play of composition. It is mass production manually crafted and composed.

China is arguably responsible for the proliferation of the low-cost industrially mass-produced object throughout the world. When we were asked to design a building in Shantou, China, for the New York-based fashion company, Lafayette 148, the issue of human labor in relation to industrially mass-produced objects was paramount. As sister industries, both clothing manufacturing and building production stem from manual crafting that progressively became less manual and more rationalized over time. We decided that it was important to make a building that took shape from human labor, rather than a building whose primary vocabulary was assembled from industrially manufactured components. In this sense, the architectural project was, from the start, woven into questions of manual crafting, the logic of mass-production, and the tension that exists in both industries as they negotiate these modes of production.

Anyone involved in the contemporary practice of architecture knows that without mass production and repetitive manufacturing no building is feasible in today's economy. Perhaps small, unique custom-made artifacts are possible, but at the scale of an eleven-story factory, a completely hand-crafted building was simply out of the question. Our aim was to critically develop a design that would speak to this tension – where manual crafting is highlighted while working with logics of mass-production. This, in fact, became possible, and maybe even heightened, in a city like Shantou. The option to build purely with rationalized systems was common-place in other major metropolitan areas of China. In Shantou, however, the abundance of labor, pushed the building industry to construct in-situ, essentially without the advantage of prefabricated parts, transported and assembled. In effect, we worked with common local building practices and tried to heighten the level of technical and constructive expertise and aesthetic discourse to extremes.

Most large scale structures in China are made of concrete, so there is nothing revolutionary in our choice to work with this material. Much of the concrete buildings in Shantou, however, are of very low grade that are subsequently covered in tiles, stone, or stucco. **(Figures 1, 2)** We decided to take on this issue as a criterion: concrete would always be left visible, and most importantly, we would push the methods of forming concrete to an extreme – of technical expertise and labor intensity. This, once again, raised the issue of labor practices, but also brought about a criticality in the question of technique and technology.

In the clothing and fashion industries, "mass-customization" is a term used to describe a process that includes a mass-produced platform that hosts unique, bespoke, parts. For example a watch manufacturer may mass-produce a basic watch platform that has a customizable face, band, hands, or color. Or a shoe manufacturer may permit the selection of fabrics, colors, stitching, sole and laces as personalization of a basic shoe platform. Some clothing manufacturers even use specific client measurements for altering templates and produce almost bespoke garments. The lessons of "mass-customization" from the clothing industry helped us conceptualize ways that we could invent "platforms" that could be mass-produced, yet in assembly, we could hand-craft the composition of the mass-produced artifacts. We used this technique in the design of the glazing systems, the north elevation, and the sculpted wall.

1, 2_ Typical buildings in Shantou

The term "mass-customization" is also utilized in the context of architecture, where it has taken a different meaning. Given that outside of small pre-fabricated buildings, there is not a platform that may be mass-produced in architecture, "mass-customization" in buildings has meant the direct fabrication of parts from the architect's drawing files, using computationally driven tooling. This marks a new arena in the building industry that is between the hand-crafted and the mass-produced. In mass production, a singular component is made repetitively, without any change between fabricated units. With the advent of computer numerically controlled (CNC) tooling, each fabricated piece is manufactured directly from a digital file, thus providing the possibility of change from unit to unit. This, of course, would permit infinite variability among fabricated units. For example, the structural steel members of a three-dimensionally curving roof are all different. But, the shape of every one of them may be described as a set of templates that can drive a CNC mill, or laser-cutter that could manufacture each shape as if they were all repetitive and mass-produced.

In our analysis, "mass-customization," as applied to architecture, would produce variation in shape, but would always and only be experienced as if it was mass-produced. Its vocabulary belonged to mass-production. The material sensibility and singularity for which we were searching in the manually-crafted object was only possible through the introduction of human labor in the process of fabrication in such a way that the final product be marked by the labor. Mass-customization, much like mass-production, masks the effects of human labor. In effect, the criticality of the project was defined by the relationship between the mass-produced and the manually-crafted: How to create a building of spatial, aesthetic and constructive anomalies from a repetitive mass-produced set of parts. The building, architecturally, is a record of the tension between the mass-produced and the manually-crafted.

We arrived at this tension through architectural terms. But once we were there, we recognized that the manufacture of clothing, even in the mass market of today's global consumer industry enjoys this same tension between mass-production and hand-craft. At the L-148 factory, on the cutting floor, CNC cutters prepare fabric for sewing from digital files, and yet there is a worker hand linking the shoulder seams, and adding handmade stitching and beads to garments. Of course, at the scale of an eleven-story building, this level of manual crafting had to be tempered. But, nonetheless, this tension between the mass-produced and the bespoke became the critical issue in this project.
(**Figures 3-6, and 12-14, following pages**)

3-6_ Adding handmade stitching and beads to garments

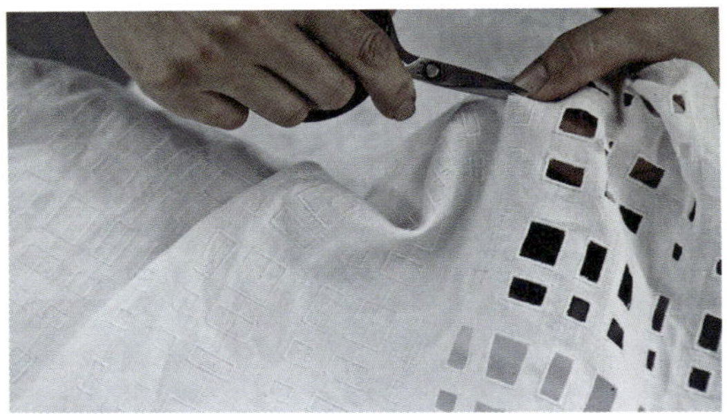
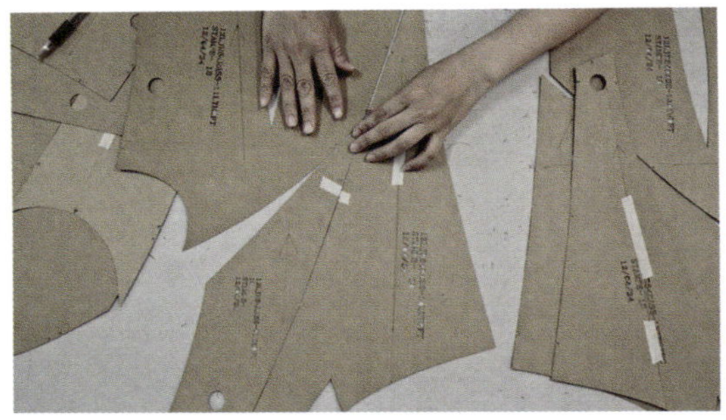

7-10_ Early studies of textiles

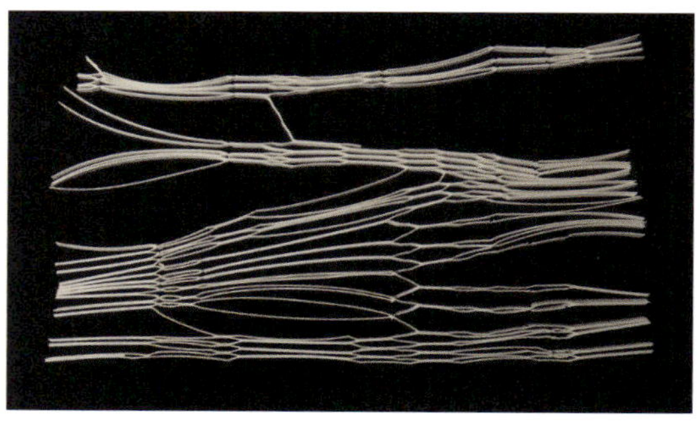

11_ Detail image of the south façade

12-14_ Adding handmade stitching and beads to garments

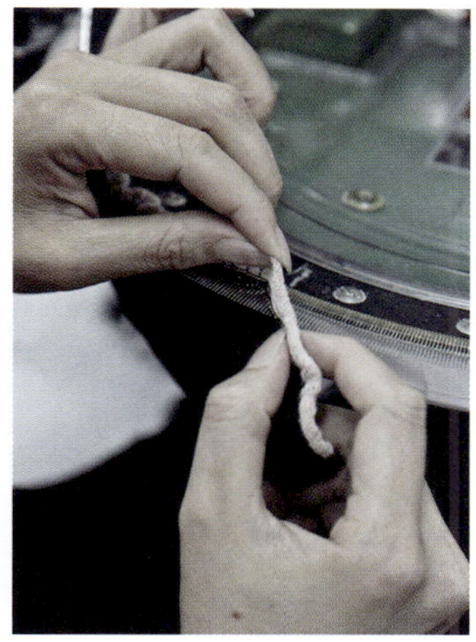

In connection to the mass-production/hand-craft dialectic, we wanted the building to reflect the relationship of its programmatic source, that of textiles and clothing production. We explored looms and weaving as sources of structural and formal configurations. **(Figures 7 - 10, opposite page)** In the production of textiles, the infrastructure of the loom regulates the organization of the produced textile, and once completed, it releases the textile, which has been indelibly marked by the infrastructure of the loom. The same loom is used to make a variety of textiles. We sought to make this link in two ways: one by creating the main façade of the building through "weaving" horizontal and vertical members together, and two, by recognizing the potential of a parallel relationship between loom/textile and formwork/concrete. **(Figure 11)** Both of these end up marking the design and the construction of the building in considerable ways. Where the two processes differ is in the ability of contemporary CNC looms to adjust warp and weft spacing in order to accommodate multitudes of textile weaves within the same loom, with infinite variability. There is a parallel attempt in the way we used the same form-work with variable angles to accommodate multiple casts.

While working on the textiles, we conducted programmatic analysis and produced a number of alternatives that engaged not only the building but also the site. Combined with zoning considerations, seismic issues, and our desire to provide an open, well-lit factory, we produced multiple variations, three of which made a set of formal proposals. Each of the three alternatives carved into the site or engaged the history of the site as a source for the building form and organization. Alternative one totally separated the services of the building in a separate slab building with bridges that connected it to the open factory building, a glazed crystalline, with a "woven" framing system for the glazing. In this proposal, we also carved the earth in order to accommodate lighting of the basement services. **(Figures 15-22, pages 22, 23)**

In alternative two, we used the history of the site as a fish hatchery and developed the infrastructure of the building based on the infrastructure of the fish hatcheries. With this proposal, we began to explore fins as shading devices on the façades of the building. **(Figures 23-30, pages 24, 25)**

In alternative three, we shaped all of the building systems and services into a u-shaped, carved umbrella that encompassed a crystalline open factory within. In this proposal, we again carved the ground to introduce daylight into the basement building services. **(Figures 31-38, pages 26, 27)** Although none of these alternatives became the final building, each played a role in the development of the project: the building services (core) on the north side of the building, a crystalline, glazed open factory, sun shading fins, carvings into the mass of the building, and day-lighting the basement.

15-22_ Model images, diagrams, and drawings of alternative 1

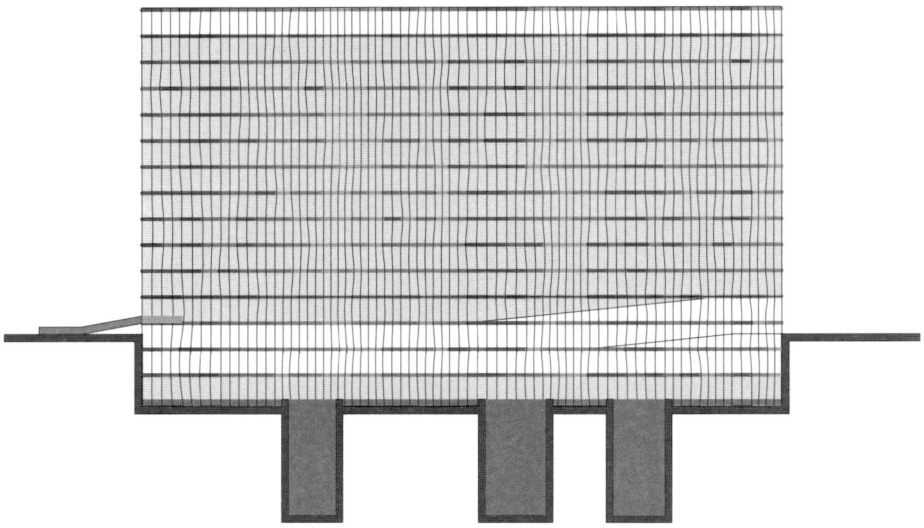

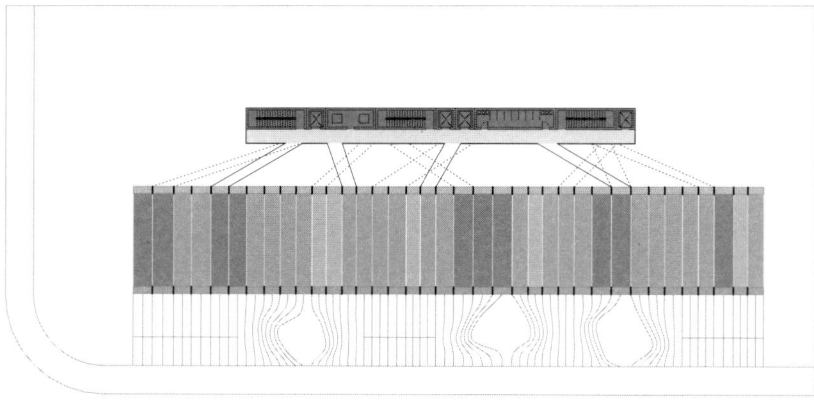

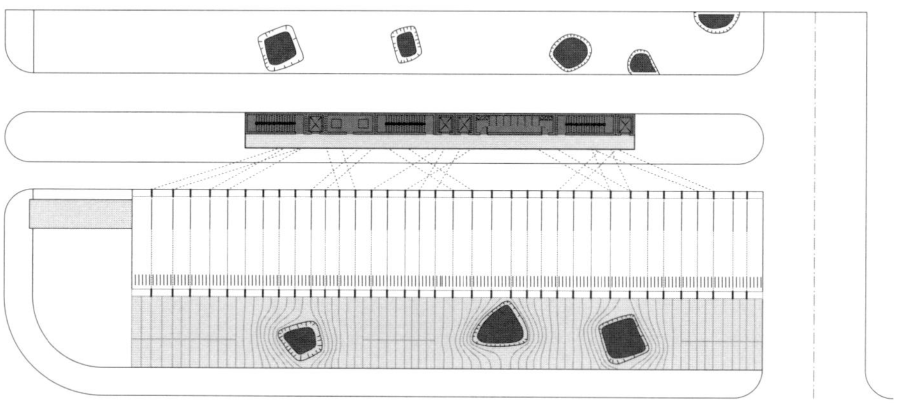

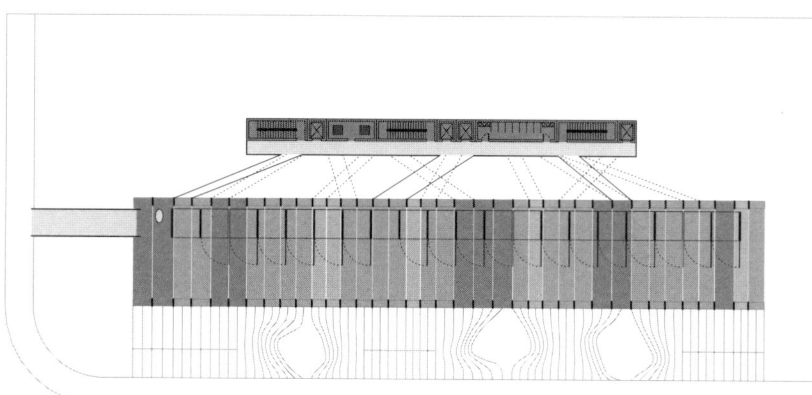

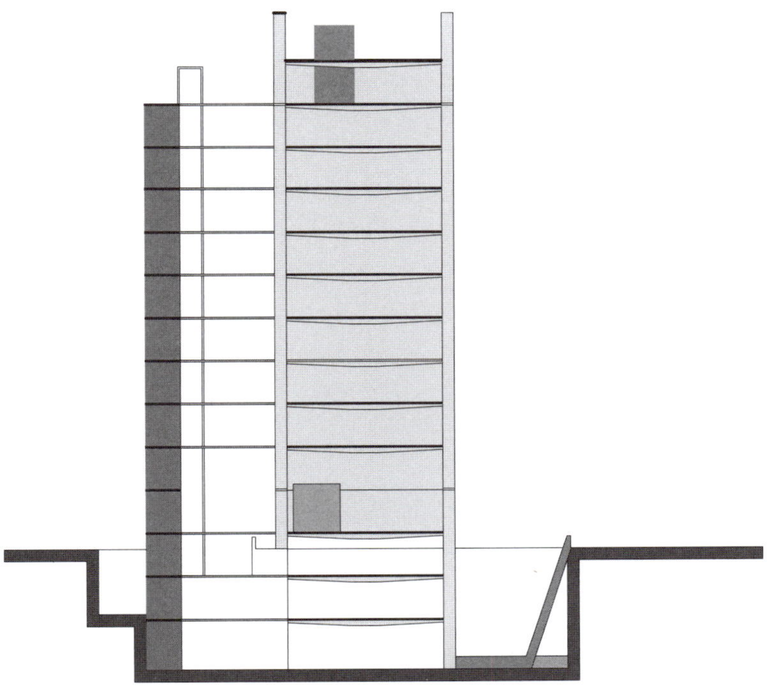

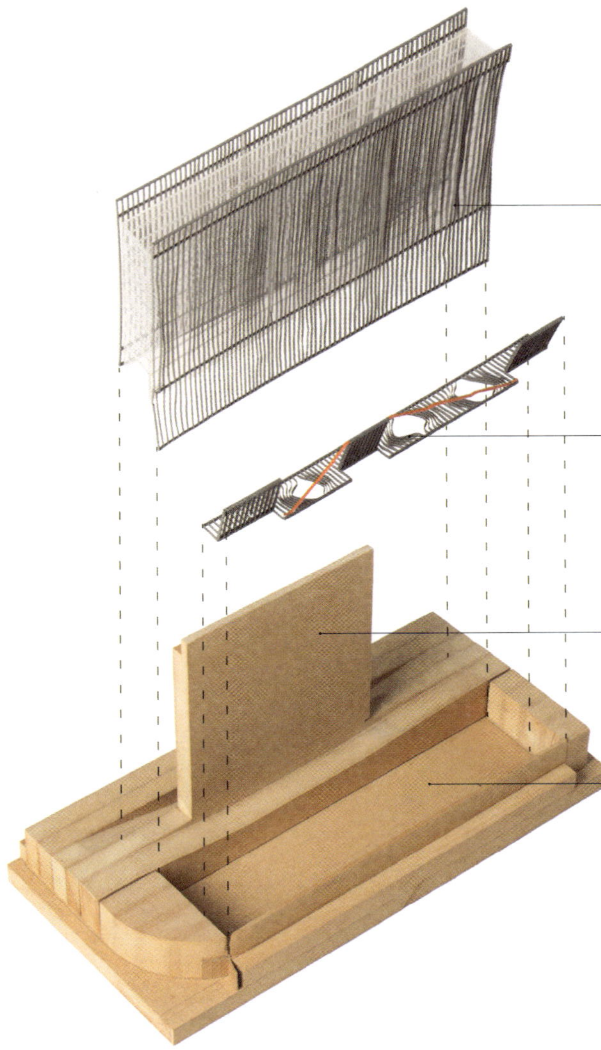
Vertical Fins +
Clear Factory Floor
Landscape Fins
Core
Parking

23-30_ Model images, diagrams, and drawings of alternative 2

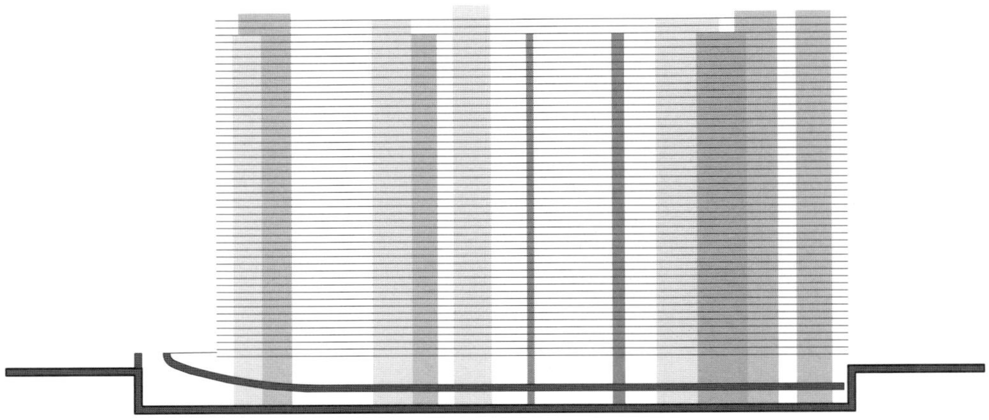

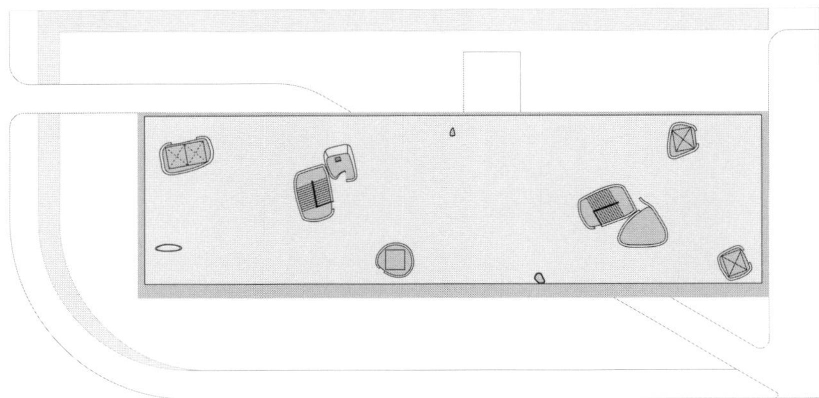

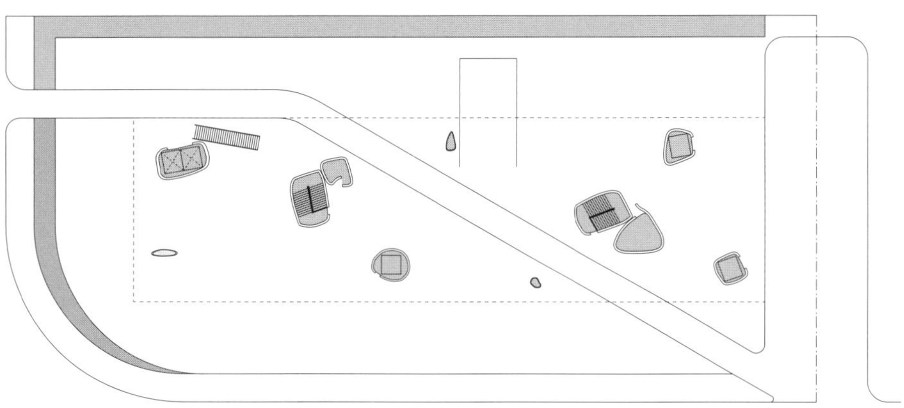

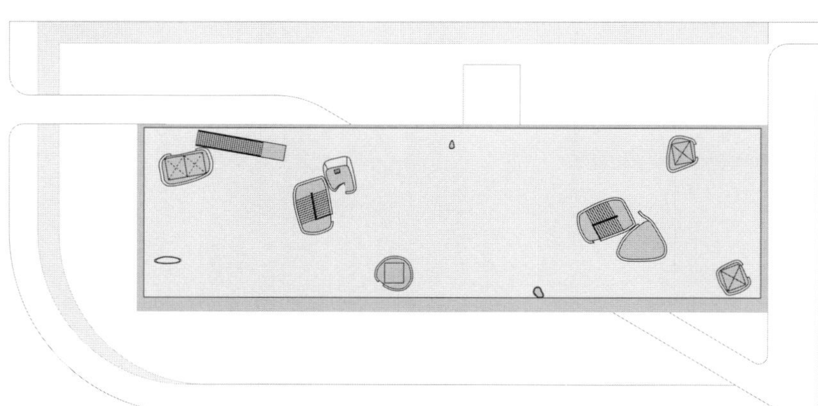

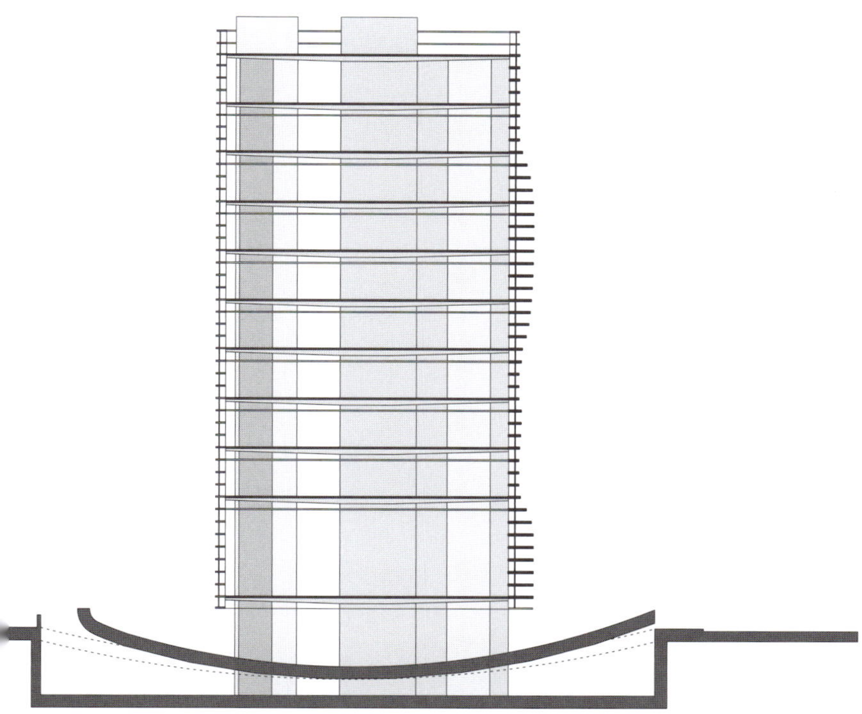

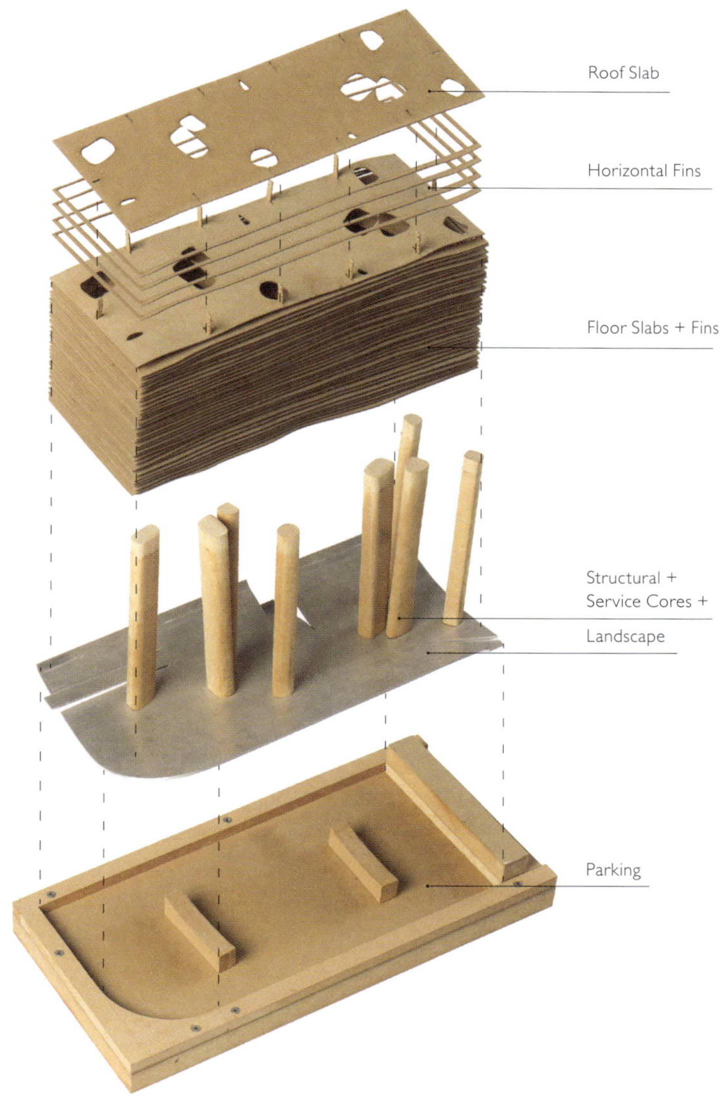
Roof Slab
Horizontal Fins
Floor Slabs + Fins
Structural +
Service Cores +
Landscape
Parking

31-38_ Model images, diagrams, and drawings of alternative 3

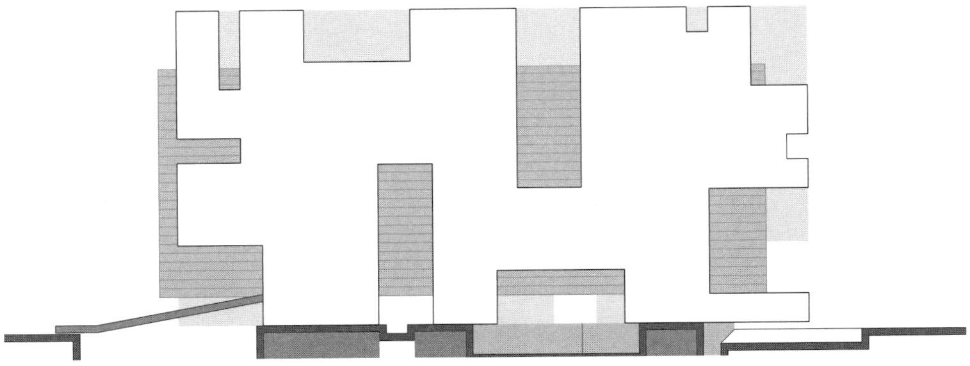

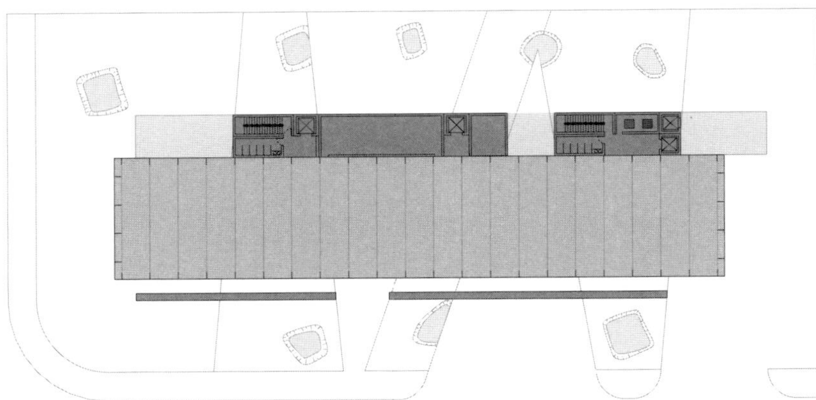

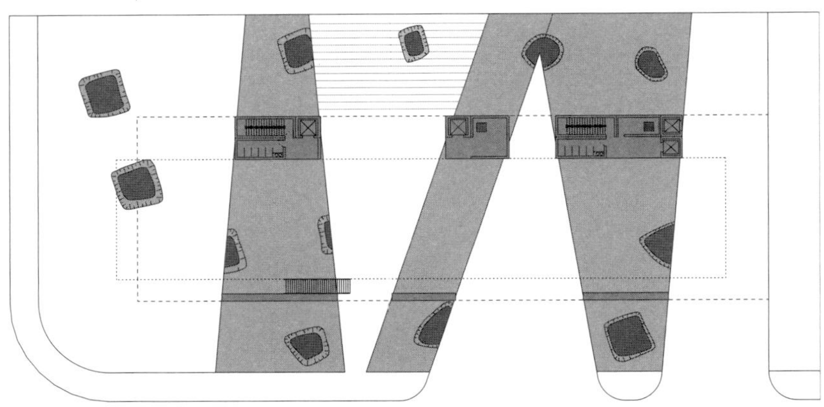

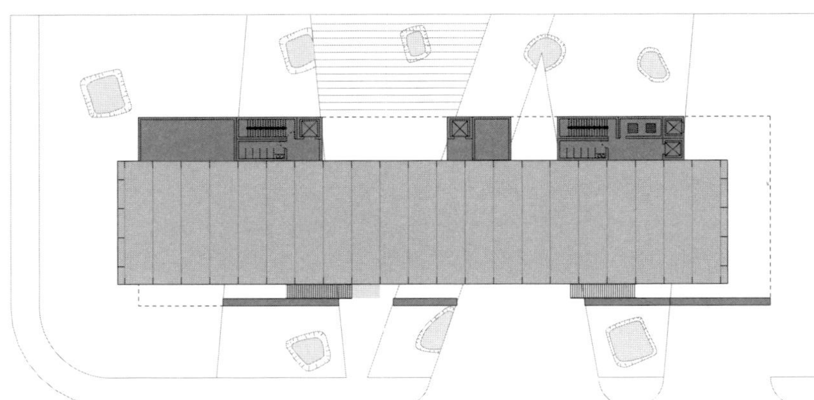

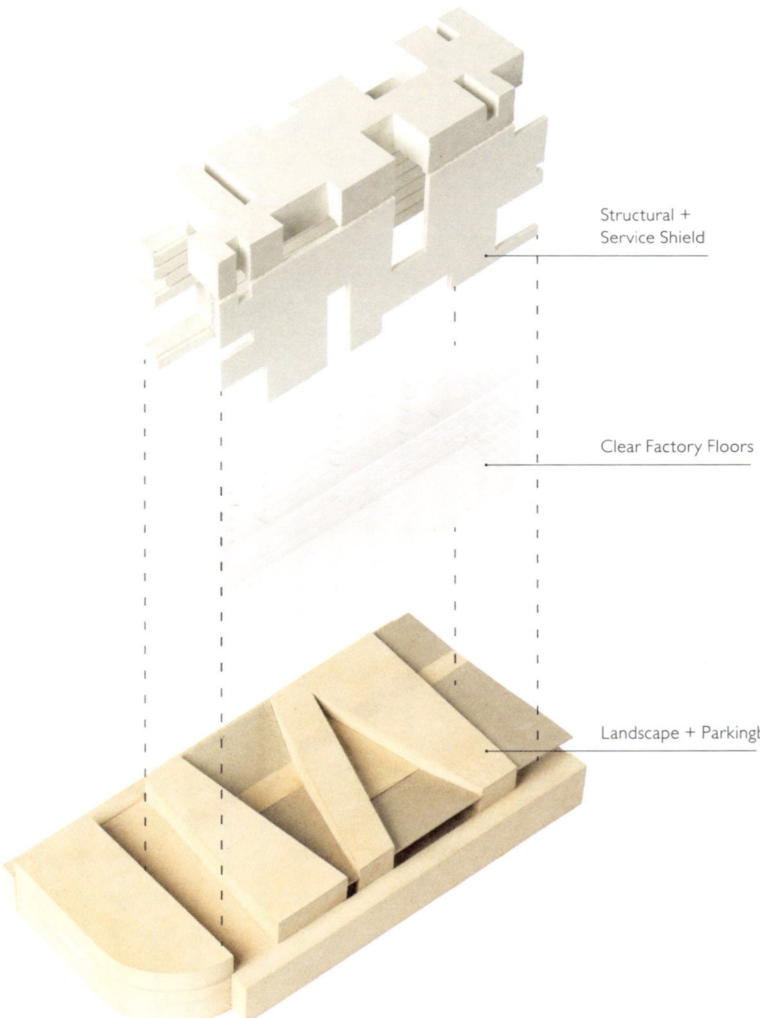
Structural +
Service Shield
Clear Factory Floors
Landscape + Parkingb

Interlude
Brian Carter

Textiles, Machines, Flow and Factories

"only here... the machinery and buildings can be found commensurate with the miracle of modern times – they are called factories."
Karl Freidrich Schinkel

Making textiles was, for centuries, a cottage industry. The pervasive domestic activity, invariably modest in scale and historically embedded in villages across the world, was signaled by the clatter of looms and identifiable, in certain places, only by long horizontal strips of windows tucked under the eaves of houses. New machines brought radical change. The flying shuttle, devised by John Kay in 1733, was quickly followed by other inventions. The spinning jenny, the shuttle drop box and Crompton's spinning mule were all in use by 1780 and, together with the people who operated them and sudden increases in the flow of raw materials and finished goods, those machines prompted a need for other spaces – spaces that were expansive, open, and lofty. The new machines also needed power and, as a consequence, spaces were constructed close to reliable sources that could be readily harnessed. Together these requirements combined to generate the design of strikingly different buildings.

Speculating on the form and appearance of these new buildings, the French architect Francois Blondel, writing in his *Cours d'architecture* of 1771, suggested that the factory, or *manufacture*, should look simple and solid and be built on the periphery of a town by a river.[1] Almost twenty years later, Francesco Milizia, outlining his *Principi di architettura civile* reiterated that *manufattorie* should be simple and proud.[2] Characterized by the rational ordering of space, limited palettes of materials, and explicit systems of construction, the first factories echoed those ideas of simplicity, solidity, and pride.

Cromford Mill was constructed in 1771 to house the mechanized spinning of cotton. The large multi-story stone building, built in a remote valley in the heart of England where the damp air was conducive to working with cotton, was also close to the fast flowing Bonsall Stream and Cromford Mere Sough that provided essential sources of power. The mill, which employed more than two hundred people and included housing, was a successful venture and a few years later Richard Arkwright built another six-story mill close by. These were followed by others that were constructed farther afield where the same reliable flows of raw materials, water, machines and people ensured their success. By 1774, one of Arkwright's mills near Manchester had a workforce of more than five-hundred.

The design and construction of new machines prompted the development of materials and advanced manufacturing. These materials and techniques, including the making of steel and glass and the casting of iron, had wider impacts and many were adopted to make new components and systems for buildings. Construction was transformed as industrialists, architects, engineers, and inventors devised structural columns of cast-iron, wrought iron beams, new techniques for manufacturing glass, steam engines, and systems for heating, lighting, and ventilation. All were rapidly introduced into the new factories. A six-story mill, designed for William Strutt and completed in 1797, was one of the earliest industrial buildings to use cast-iron as a structural material. Slim cruciform cast-iron columns made it possible to create large spaces within the masonry building to house machines while beams supporting brick vaulted floors, created long spans and resisted fire - addressing significant problems in buildings constructed out of timber.

Matthew Boulton and James Watt designed the Twist Mill at Salford near Manchester in 1799. When the building was completed in 1801 it had

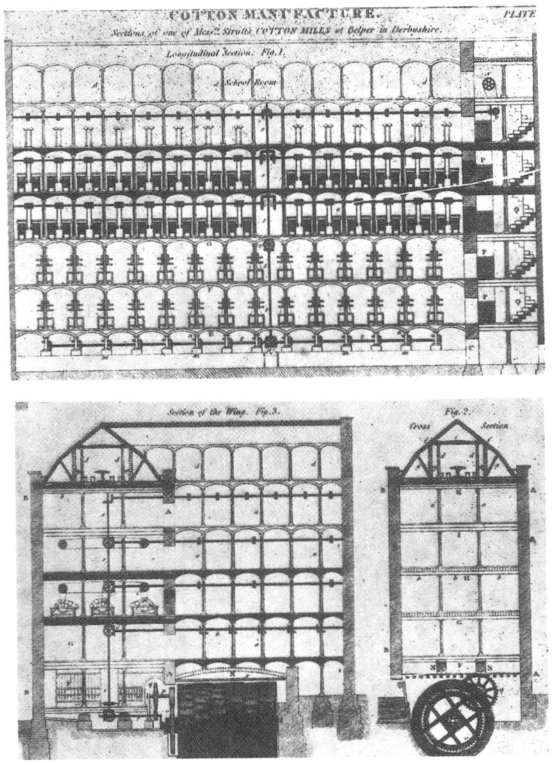

1_ Section drawings of North Mill, Belper. The production is organized on four floors over a large water wheel and spaces where power can be converted to the mechanical drives for the machines above. Cotton spinning machines are arranged in fifteen bays, each of a consistent size and coordinated with overhead mechanical drives. The design of the building demonstrates a thorough integration of structural, mechanical and operational systems.

an inner structural frame of cast-iron columns and wrought iron beams and the machines were powered by a sixty horsepower steam engine – the most powerful to have been built at that time. A central heating system was created by passing steam through the cast-iron columns and the mill was equipped with gas lighting. Twist Mill was not only a new building designed to house machines but a building that was itself transforming into a machine.

Construction systems, machines and power became increasingly integrated. The drawings of North Mill – a factory for 'cotton manufacture' designed for William Strutt in 1803 – depicted a lofty four story building constructed above a large waterwheel.[3] **(Figure 1)** The structural module was developed to maximize the potential strengths of materials while also taking account of the layout of machines. The entire building was dimensionally coordinated and spatially organized to house people and machines efficiently as well as accommodating the mechanical drives that converted water power and enabled production.

After visiting mills in Manchester in 1826 the head of Prussia's Department of Trade, suggested to his colleague, the Privy Counselor for Public Works, that "only here... the machinery and buildings can be found commensurate with the miracles of modern times – they are called factories." Subsequently that colleague, Karl Friedrich Schinkel, travelled to see the buildings for himself. During his visit he looked carefully at the use of brick and cast-iron, scribbled notes and made drawings of the monumental factories – references that informed Schinkel's development of a new, yet historically grounded, approach to architectural design that was to become an international style.

The Transparent Shed

New technological developments and the increased use of steel, iron, glass, and prefabricated components shaped the vast transparent shed designed by Joseph Paxton to house the Great Exhibition of 1851 in London. While this building was not a factory it was filled with machines and a remarkable collection of things made by machines. The exhibition attracted people from across the world and while the building radically transformed perceptions of space, construction and enclosure of the artifacts on display highlighted the potential of increasingly fast flowing industrial production. Gottfried Semper's visit to the Great Exhibition, however, focused on a small Caribbean hut. Captivated by this modest structure he went on to contemplate the design and origins of shelter by identifying four essential elements – the hearth, platform, roof, and enclosure – considerations that were to become the basis for his development of a significant theory of architecture.

In speculating on the origins of shelter and theorizing about the beginnings of architecture, Semper highlighted the significance of woven walls and the nomadic tent. Textiles and weaving had long influenced architecture while tents and pavilions were to be recognized as "magnificent structures" and "the pride of monarchs of Western Asia for thousands of years."[5] And while shelters made by the Berbers from black goats' wool, contrasted with the finely woven tapestries that adorned the walls of ancient houses across Europe and Asia, together they demonstrated the significance of textiles in architecture and their potential to provide shelter, comfort, and decoration in widely different settings and cultures. These qualities and the characteristics of carefully

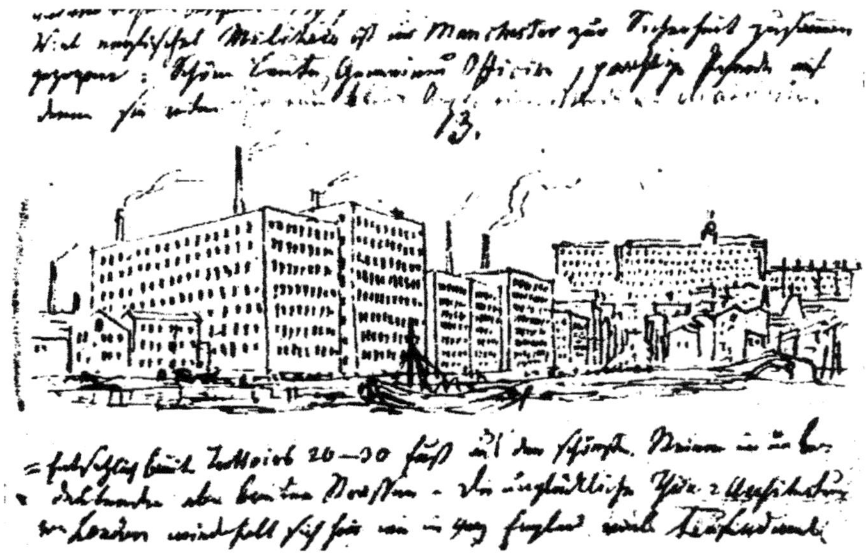

2_ Notes and sketches of factories and mills in Manchester by Schinkel. On his visit to Manchester in 1826 Karl Friedrich Schinkel made extensive notes and drawings of the new mill buildings between 16 July and 18 July.

designed and intricately spun, braided and woven textiles captured the imagination of craftsmen, architects, and critics. Subsequently, Semper's treatises were to be combined with Schinkel's considerations of order, proportion, and materials, to suggest spectacle and theatricality – concepts that continue to influence contemporary architecture. **(Figure 2)**

Flow and Factories

As free flowing cast-iron shaped the factory in the eighteenth century so concrete was to inspire its form and construction a hundred years later. This liquid material, literally poured into place, offered opportunities to create significant structures and explore plasticity and form. And, with the addition of finely woven threads of steel reinforcement, the flowing material, strong in both compression and tension, was used to create long spans and define large spaces while offering sculpted lightness. These were significant advantages that would be explored to serve the changing needs of industry and industrialists. In 1892 the French engineer François Hennebique obtained a patent for a new system of floor construction. Utilizing monolithic reinforced concrete, this system provided greater load bearing capacity and improved fire-proofing between floors while resisting vibration and humidity. Hennebique went on to refine these techniques in his designs for new factories for textile companies in France. One of those buildings, a four-story block planned to house the Charles VI spinning mill at Tourcoing completed in 1894, was designed with a clearly expressed frame in-filled with expansive windows to create generous, open and well-lit workspaces within the austere reinforced concrete structure.

A few years later, Auguste Perret, an architect who was also pre-occupied with concrete, lightness, and light, designed a reinforced concrete structure of parabolic arches for a new clothing factory for Edsers in Paris. **(Figure 3, page 34)** By utilizing the inherent qualities of the material, he was able to minimize the size of structural members and create a remarkably light enclosure that defined an impressive three-story high workroom. This space, surrounded by a series of galleries housing additional workspaces, was flooded with daylight from a roof made almost entirely of glass.

Good lighting was frequently demanded by industrialists in order to accommodate activities that relied on detailed hand work, precision and assembly and when Building No.10 – a two-story workshop planned for the Packard Motor Company in Detroit – opened in 1905, it was defined as a "Daylight Factory." Designed by the architect Albert Kahn, this building had an exposed concrete frame that was in-filled by large windows and provided open interior spaces defined by grids of columns. It recalled the factory at Tourcoing designed by Hennebique a few years earlier and developed similar spaces that were light and open. Defined by grids of columns, those internal spaces were also to prove as effective for making cars as for spinning cotton. The building for Packard attracted the attention of other industrialists and Albert Kahn was subsequently commissioned to design factories in America for companies making products that ranged from cars and gears to adding machines, pharmaceuticals and linotype. However when Kahn was invited to design a new factory in Detroit in 1909, it was a request to create appropriate spaces to build the Ford Model T – arguably the ultimate machine of the time.

Albert Kahn designed a factory for Ford that provided space for a new assembly workshop on an urban site at Highland Park in Detroit. More than eight hundred feet long and planned on four

3_ Atelier Esders, Paris. In his design for this new clothing factory, prepared in 1908, Auguste Perret sought to reduce the reinforced concrete structure to a minimum and emphasize lightness. The lightness of the structure in turn enabled the incorporation of a glass roof to bring generous amounts of daylight into the workspaces.

levels, the building had large windows set within a reinforced concrete frame structure that created expansive, open floors and well-lit workspaces. Those spaces were planned to accommodate the long and rapidly growing assembly lines that Ford was developing, which would defined car production for the auto industry more broadly. Hydraulic freight elevators, stairs, and changing rooms for staff were housed in towers that were located alongside yet separated from the workspace so as not to impede the vital flows of production. Highland Park was a vast new factory and its design assertively underlined the importance of efficiency in space and time. The building, which presented a long glazed façade topped with story high lettering signing the Ford Motor Company on Woodward Avenue in the heart of the city, opened on January 1, 1910.

At the same time that he was working on the design of these buildings Albert Kahn also collaborated with his brothers Julius and Moritz in search to find ways of making the construction of reinforced concrete more efficient. Inspired by the research of Julius Kahn, an engineer, and experiences working with concrete, they devised "Truscon" – a unique form of steel reinforcement. It combined previously separate pieces of steel into a single unit. Easily prefabricated and readily placed during construction, it reduced labor and the time demanded by conventional constructional techniques based on weaving together complex three-dimensional fabrics of steel reinforcement rods prior to the pouring of the concrete. The particular approach that Kahn and his brothers developed for the production and placement of steel reinforcement was adopted enthusiastically by industry and, in 1905, Julius Kahn became the first President of the Trussed Concrete Steel Company when it was established in the United States to fabricate and market the new building product.

While many architects working in practice at this time viewed the design of industrial buildings with disdain, Albert Kahn continued to seek out opportunities to create new factories. Based on his experiences he also initiated a new model of professional practice by bringing together all of the disciplines involved with the design and construction of buildings. It was a response that sought to capitalize on efficiencies and, contrary to conventional patterns of practice, focused on harnessing the potential of interdisciplinary teams of architects, structural and environmental engineers, cost estimators, and construction specialists working together in the same office. In that setting they not only had opportunities to develop designs for buildings that integrated systems of structure, enclosure, and environmental servicing but could also coordinate those systems with the selection of materials, sequences of construction, and the control of building costs to ensure the efficient delivery of information and buildings. This particularly creative way of working, radically different from conventional architectural practice, was prompted by the design of the factory.

The quest for efficiency in factories required the ordered supply of raw materials, smooth flows of work, and timely dispatch of finished products. Frederick W. Taylor – a former factory worker at the Midvale Steel Company in Philadelphia – became obsessed by the need for industrial processes to flow smoothly. He studied working methods and their impact on production and carried out research that generated a number of articles between 1894 and 1906. However it was the publication of Taylor's book *The Principles of Scientific Management* in 1911 that was to project ideas of scientific management into industry, design, and construction. The book attracted attention and became increasingly influential in the planning and design of factories. Outlining the need for spaces to accommodate the easy movement of goods, people, and things, it highlighted how improved flows could make industrial processes, and the factories that housed them, more efficient while improving quality and profitability. At the same time Henry Ford, a pioneer in the development of the industrial production line, continued to focus his attention on the benefits of organization and efficiency and their influence of the design of new factories.

Transatlantic Flows

During this time the "Trussed Concrete Steel Company" became increasingly successful and, together with his brothers, Albert Kahn initiated an international network to market "Truscon." Moritz Kahn led the company that was established in London in 1907 and Owen Williams, a young structural engineer, was hired to promote the system in the United Kingdom. Multi-story factories utilizing the "Truscon" system of reinforcement in clearly expressed concrete frames were designed and built in Birmingham and London while a five-story building, planned to house a Garments Factory for "Viyella" in Nottingham, was completed in 1919. That building in England's East Midlands, perhaps not surprisingly, closely resembled the austere "Daylight Factories" designed by Albert Kahn a few years earlier in America's mid-west.

Owen Williams was subsequently commissioned to design another new industrial complex a few miles from the "Viyella" Garment Factory. The building that he designed for Boots at Beeston, constructed almost entirely of reinforced concrete, opened in 1931. D10 – a four-story factory – was planned to accommodate twelve hundred people and house the manufacture of a range of pharmaceutical products – liquid medicines, creams, toothpaste, and perfumes – together with space for management staff, laboratories, and canteens. Built of reinforced concrete, the structure, which consisted of mushroom-head columns and flat slabs, was wrapped in a sheer skin of glass. As a result the plastic forms of the concrete structure were clearly visible by day and night. The strikingly transparent complex was organized around a series of vast top lit work spaces. Each of these spaces was planned to bring natural light into the heart of the building and at the same time, enable the easy movement of raw materials, production, packaging and finished products. The organization of day lit spaces that enhanced flows through the building created good workplaces and realized efficiencies and, with the completion of the new factory, Boots produced a manufacturing surplus that enabled the company to be the first in the UK to reduce the working week to five days with no reduction in the pay of workers. Productivity continued to increase, absenteeism reduced, and eventually the five day working week initiated by Boots at Beeston became an industry norm throughout the United Kingdom.

The Material of Modernism

Nikolaus Pevsner defined the new factory that was designed for Boots by Owen Williams as "a milestone in modern architecture and especially concrete architecture"[6] – a statement that highlighted the significant relationship between modernism and concrete. That relationship had been emphasized by Le Corbusier whose influential drawing of the Dom-Ino House had been published in 1915. Simultaneously his enthusiasm, and that of the European modernists, had been captured by images of other reinforced concrete structures designed for industry to make both the rational grids of daylight factories and the sculptural forms of grain elevators in Buffalo and Buenos Aires inspirations for the advancement of modernism.

Awareness of those different forms and the contributions of engineers created a widening interest in reinforced concrete and its use for new buildings in the first half of the twentieth century. And, as buildings in North America became an inspiration to architects in Europe, so they prompted other designers in Asia and South America. Niemeyer, Raymond, Candela, Nervi, Costa represented just a few of the architects and engineers who went on to explore the potential and plasticity of reinforced concrete internationally and whose work advanced innovative systems of fabrication, structural form, and the design of new concrete buildings that were responsive to climate.

New Modernism

Perhaps it is hardly surprising that the design for a new factory in the twenty-first century to be built in China was envisaged as a concrete building. Located in the country that produces more than half of the world's cement, China was also the largest consumer of concrete per capita globally when L-148 was commissioned (between 1973 and 2004 China's consumption of concrete increased from 25 to 430 kg. whilst over the same period consumption in the USA remained almost constant at 350kg per head).[7] And, while much of the concrete that was being used in China at this time was directed to the construction of large infrastructure projects it advanced expertise and technical sophistication amongst local engineers, contractors, and fabricators. At the same time that the designers of L-148 became aware of the high quality of concrete work in new infrastructural projects, they also detected a contrast in the way that the material was used to build buildings. In the majority of those new buildings in China, the quality and finish of the concrete seemed to be less of a priority and it was almost inevitably concealed by cladding. However with a particular interest in the potential of the material, and inspired by the ways that reinforced concrete had been used by the pioneers of twentieth century modernism, the designers of L-148 sought to explore the inherent qualities of the material.

Capitalizing on the skills of indigenous concrete workers in China, and collaborating with local engineers who had gained experience in the construction of large-scale infrastructural projects, they were able to develop techniques for pre-casting and prefabrication as well as the development of concrete mixes and high quality finishes during the design and construction of the building. The designers also sought to develop reinforced concrete elements that could be made by hand so as to capitalize on the newly acquired skills of construction workers and engineers while at the same time referencing the significance of craft and value of human skills in both construction and the textile industry.

The frame of this new factory consists of horizontally and vertically reinforced site cast concrete members. Once assembled these elements are post tensioned to create a primary structure that recalls a woven fabric. In addition, a unique system of external cladding was developed for the project. Consisting of specially designed reinforced concrete horizontal louvers system that creates an external screen which shades the south, west, and east facing glazed walls of the new industrial workspaces. In addition the louvers are perforated, so as to provide privacy while offering views out from the workrooms, and twisted in order to induce natural ventilation and the flow of air through the building.

This external skin of finely formed, curving and perforate reinforced concrete louvers, recognizes the need for shade, views and ventilation and creates a vast rippling wall that signals different requirements within the building. It is a device that, in projecting a view of this new factory as a machine, recalls the Twist Mill developed by Boulton and Watt more than two hundred years earlier. The design and planning of L-148 also builds on other historical precedents. Rationally organized to create large open factory floors, the factory is served by a discrete service core housing stairs, elevators, and amenities for staff. Consequently the organization of spaces within the building responds to a familiar need for efficient flows of materials,

4_ Albert Kahn in his office, Detroit, July 12, 1938. The architect worked closely with his brothers Julius and Moritz, and subsequently developed a large multi-disciplinary practice that continues to work internationally and develop design proposals that integrate architectural concepts, structure and environmental systems.

people, and production in factories that clearly references historical precedents embedded in the early proposals of Arkwright, Boulton and Watt, and advanced by Le Corbusier, Albert Kahn and others. **(Figure 4)**

Like the first factory designed by Albert Kahn for Henry Ford in Detroit, L-148 has been built in the heart of the city. Occupying a site in the commercial center of Shantou, a port with a population of almost 4 million people, this new industrial headquarters is located alongside public and governmental agencies, commercial offices, shopping, housing and recreational facilities. In this distinctly urban setting the new eleven-story factory presents a monumental spectacle that recalls the mills in the skyline of Manchester which captured Schinkel's attention and inspired new approaches to design in architecture.

This new factory has also been conceived as an integral part of the community. Reflecting the intentions of a client who was enthusiastic to look beyond considerations of efficiency and production, the building accommodates a mix of uses. In addition to housing a range of facilities required specifically for the design, production, sales and marketing of clothing – studios, offices and workshops, a showroom, and fashion runways. Like that early factory in Cromford and subsequent developments at Saltaire and New Lanark, where industrialists Titus Salt and Robert Owen created communities around new factories, L-148 integrates design, manufacture, and in earlier design schemes, to include education and living to create a working community in the center of the city.

L-148 also creates a monumental spectacle in the city. Its louvered façades, in addition to performing an important environmental role, recall twisted threads of material and create a rippling, white wrap around the building that brings to mind the dreamy imagery of fashion, flowing textiles and the swish of movement on the catwalk. And, like clothing when viewed through the directed lenses of film and fashion, it both conceals and reveals parts of the clad body in tantalizing ways. This new factory in Shantou is a notable marker in the landscape and the skyline of the city. It is also a memorable and appropriate sign for the company that it houses. The façade, a conspicuous textile, transforms this new factory into a kinetic device that creates memorable contemporary spectacle – one that advances the ideas of Semper and Schinkel, builds on materiality and projects the factory as one of the latest miracles of modern times.

1 François Blondel, *Cours d'architecture*, Volume II, Paris 1771, page 398.

2 Francesco Milizia, *Principi di architettura civile*, 2nd. ed., Bassano 1785, II, page 281.

3 Kurt Ackermann, *Building for Industry* (Watermark Publications (UK) Limited, 1991): 20.

4 Rosemary Hill, *'Denatured'*, London Review of Books, Vol.15 No.23. 2 December 1993.

5 Bernard Rudofsky, *Architecture without architects* (The Museum of Modern Art, 1964): 45.

6 N.Pevsner, *Buildings of England: Nottinghamshire* (London, Penguin, 1951): 143.

7 A. Forty, *Concrete and Culture, A Material History* (London, Reaktion Books, 2012): 118.

Carving

Mehrdad Hadighi

Twisted for L-148 was produced for Lafayette 148 New York, a privately owned, New York-based, clothing designer and producer. Lafayette 148 had moved most of their manufacturing to Shantou, China, while maintaining some manufacturing, the design facilities, sample production, and the showroom in New York City. They commissioned us to design a 21,000 m^2 building for them in Shantou, within an urban, industrial zone, to accommodate all of their different programmatic needs. The building incorporates the design studios, showroom, sample production, administrative offices, the factory, dining halls, and a school for children of workers, in addition to parking and service spaces. Our programmatic goal was to make an open, un-interrupted, well-lit, well-ventilated work space. The factory floor was the focus, and the aim was to accommodate the factory workers in the best possible way. The program of the factory is complex due to the relationship among programmatic elements, and the multiple intersecting paths of goods and ideas. The manufacture of clothing involves the flow of goods pre and post-production and the coordination between the design process and the sequence of production. From design studio→patterning department→first sample→design studio→ patterning department→fabric warehouse→cutting department→sewing department→ pressing→storage and shipping is a linear process that is interrupted and complicated by design and decision-making processes, machine processes such as knitting and embroidery, and manual processes such as linking, beading, hand-stitching, and dying, with all of their respective delivery, storage, and independent access.

To add to this programmatic complexity, the building is in a seismically active region, governed by seismic codes. Given the length of the building, the local codes dictated two seismic joints in the buildings, in effect breaking the building into three equal volumes. **(Figures 7-9, page 47)** These joints would be experienced in the building mass as cuts that normally are covered by a flexible or sliding membrane, essentially permitting the building to act as three independent buildings. We turned these linear cuts into spatial carvings, carving into the mass of the building, creating a series of anomalous plastic outdoor spaces within the regularity of the building frame and the programmatic operations of the factory. **(Figure 10, page 48)** In addition, we utilized these carvings towards environmental ends in a few ways. First, by bringing light into the depth of the building at regular intervals, so that the entire interior may be day-lit. Next, by utilizing the openings as chimneys, sucking hot air from the factory floors towards the top of the building, thus creating a constant natural breeze in the interior environment. This air movement also helps remove textile "dust" from the interior. **(Figure 13, page 49)**

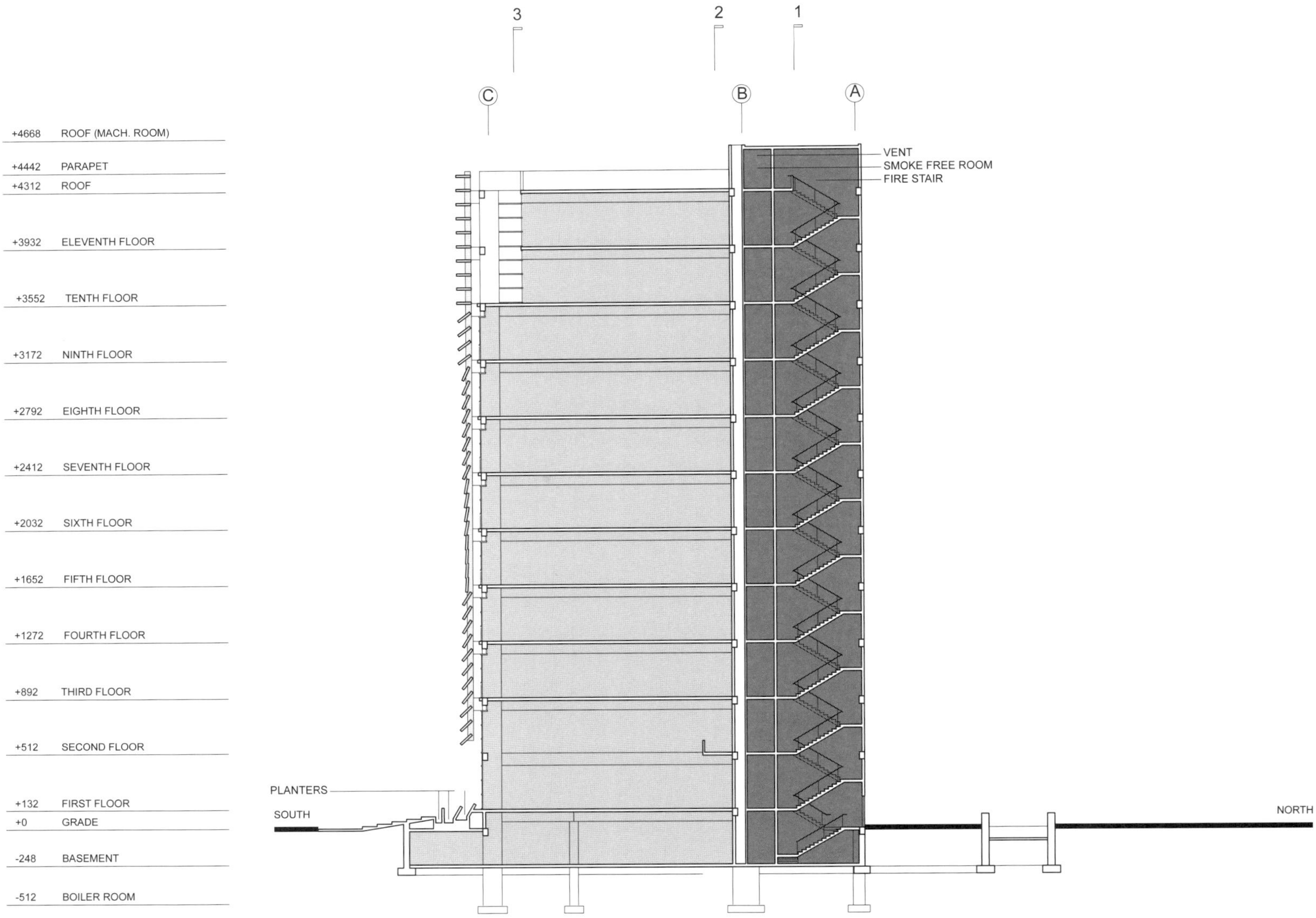

1,2_North-South sections

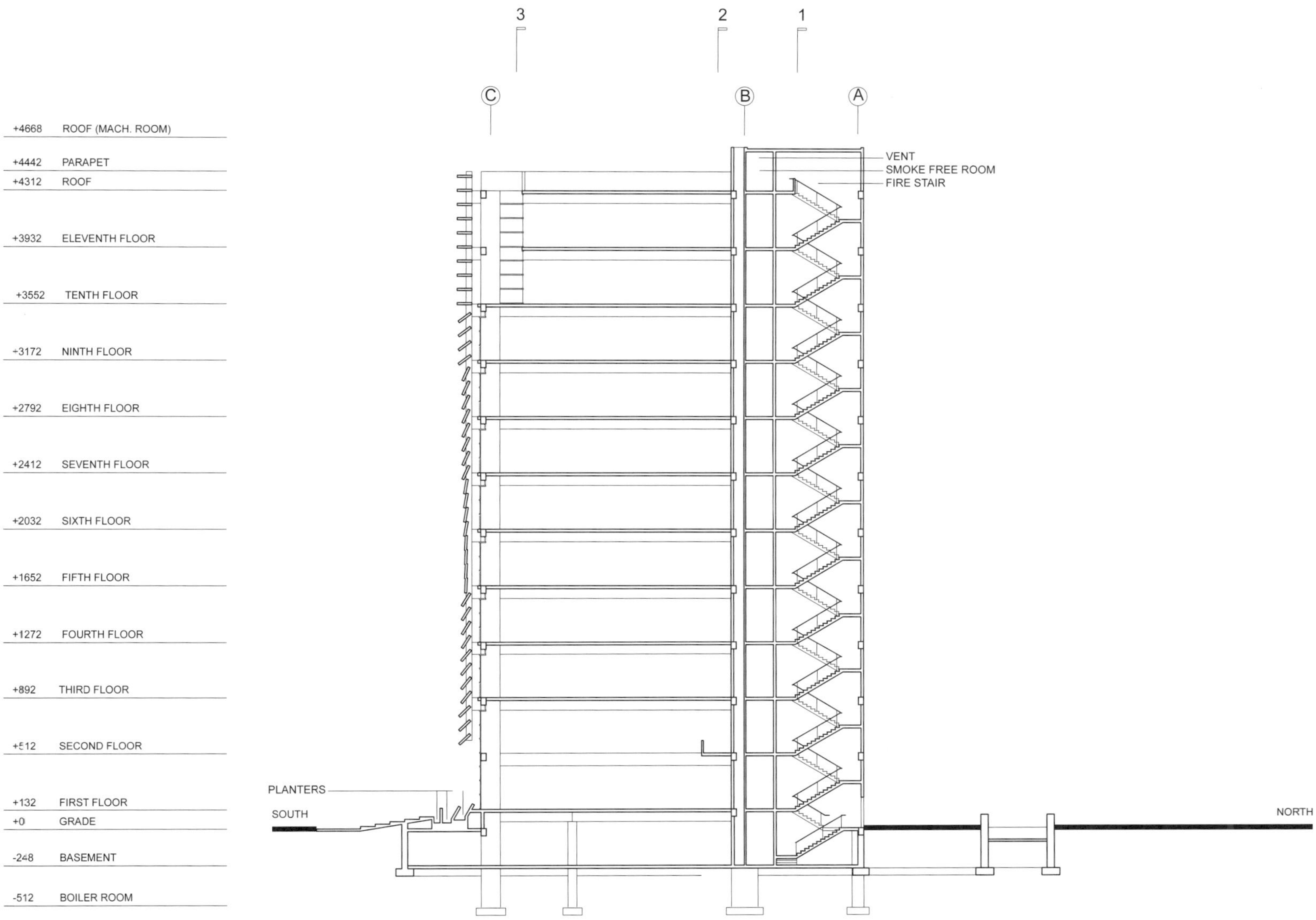
3
2
1
C
B
A
+4668 ROOF (MACH. ROOM)
+4442 PARAPET
+4312 ROOF
+3932 ELEVENTH FLOOR
+3552 TENTH FLOOR
+3172 NINTH FLOOR
+2792 EIGHTH FLOOR
+2412 SEVENTH FLOOR
+2032 SIXTH FLOOR
+1652 FIFTH FLOOR
+1272 FOURTH FLOOR
+892 THIRD FLOOR
+512 SECOND FLOOR
+132 FIRST FLOOR
+0 GRADE
-248 BASEMENT
-512 BOILER ROOM
VENT
SMOKE FREE ROOM
FIRE STAIR
PLANTERS
SOUTH
NORTH

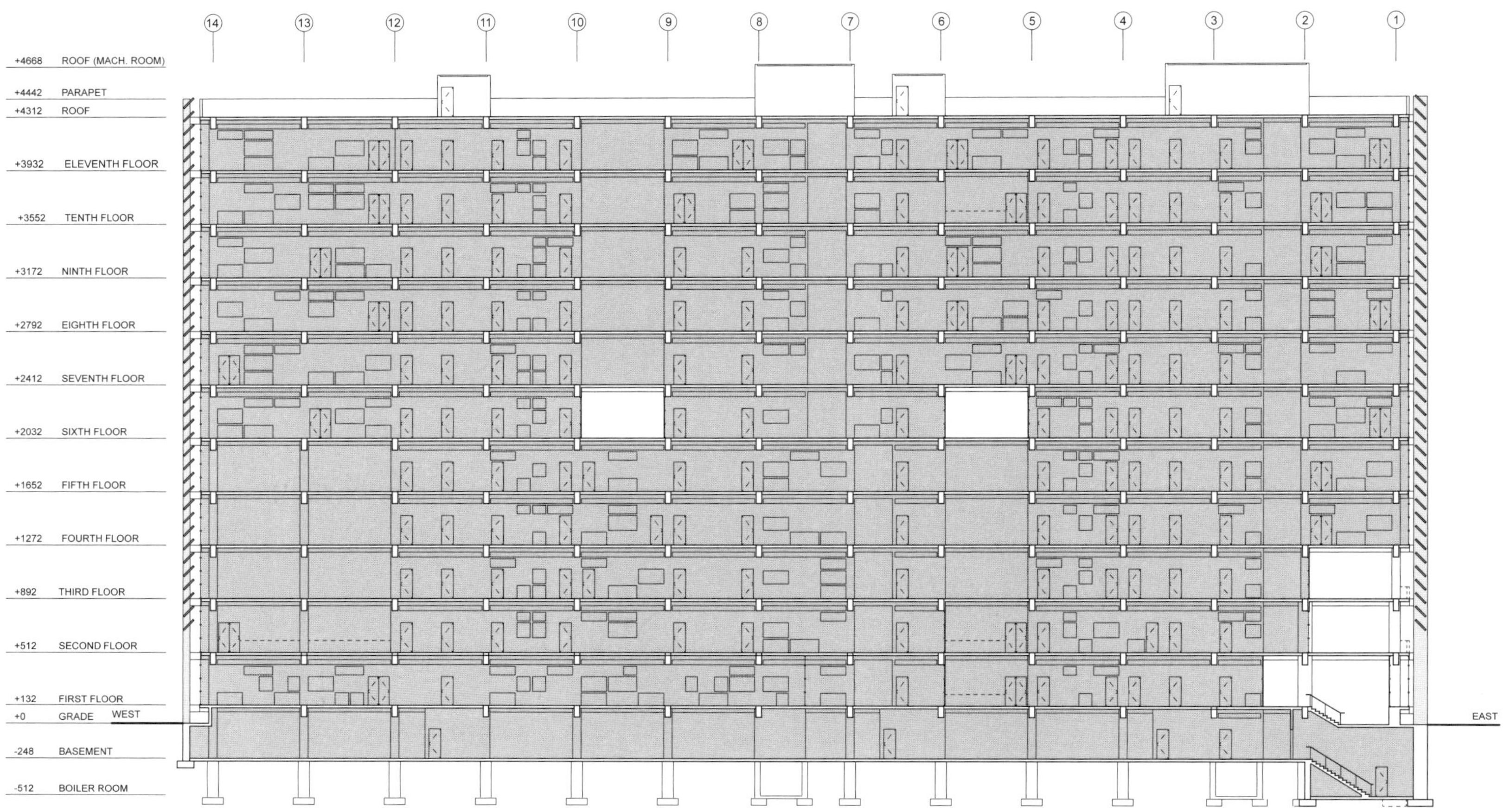

3,4_East-West sections

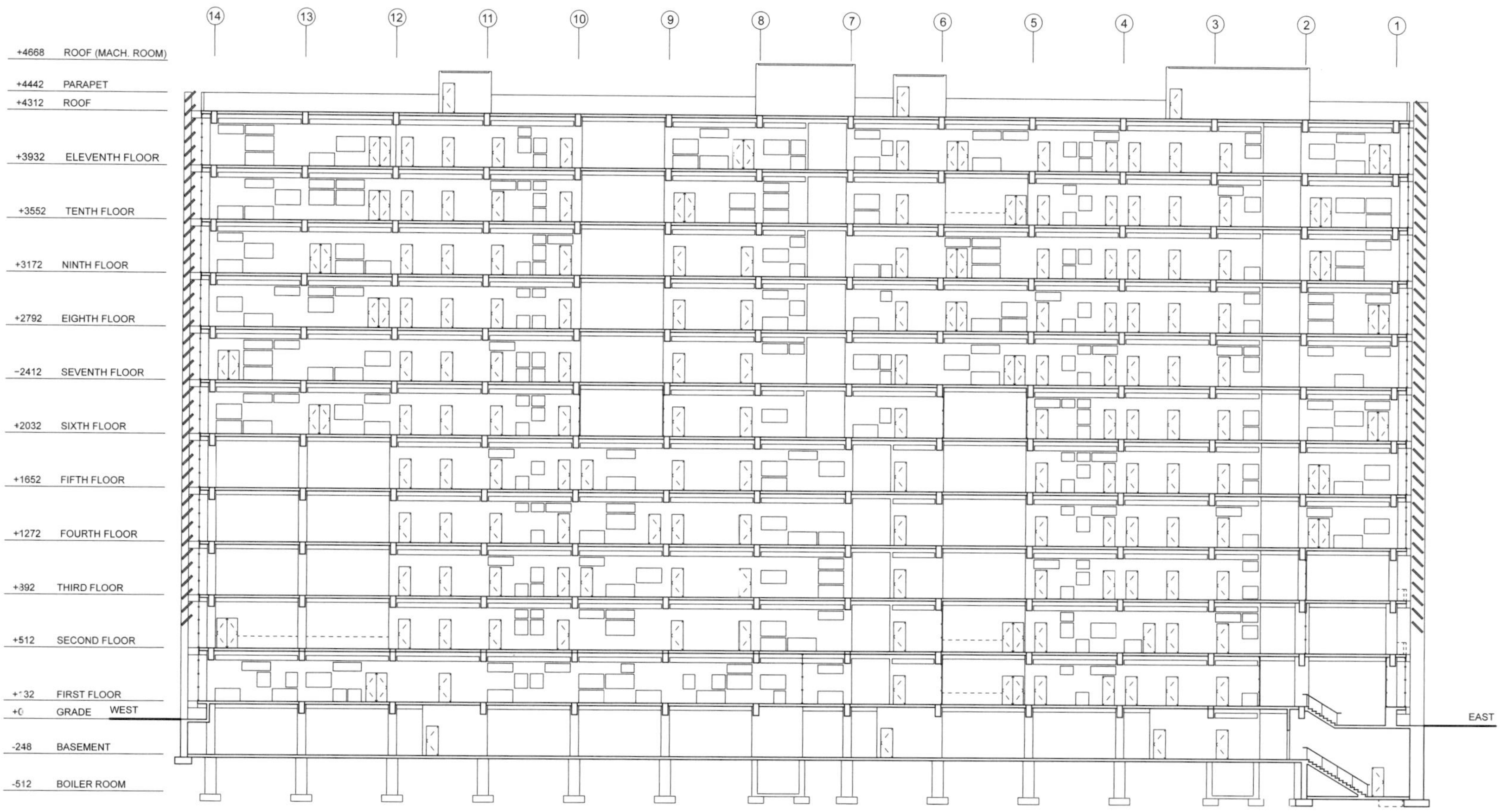

14
13
12
11
10
9
8
7
6
5
4
3
2
1
+4668 ROOF (MACH. ROOM)
+4442 PARAPET
+4312 ROOF
+3932 ELEVENTH FLOOR
+3552 TENTH FLOOR
+3172 NINTH FLOOR
+2792 EIGHTH FLOOR
-2412 SEVENTH FLOOR
+2032 SIXTH FLOOR
+1652 FIFTH FLOOR
+1272 FOURTH FLOOR
+392 THIRD FLOOR
+512 SECOND FLOOR
+132 FIRST FLOOR
+0 GRADE
WEST
EAST
-248 BASEMENT
-512 BOILER ROOM

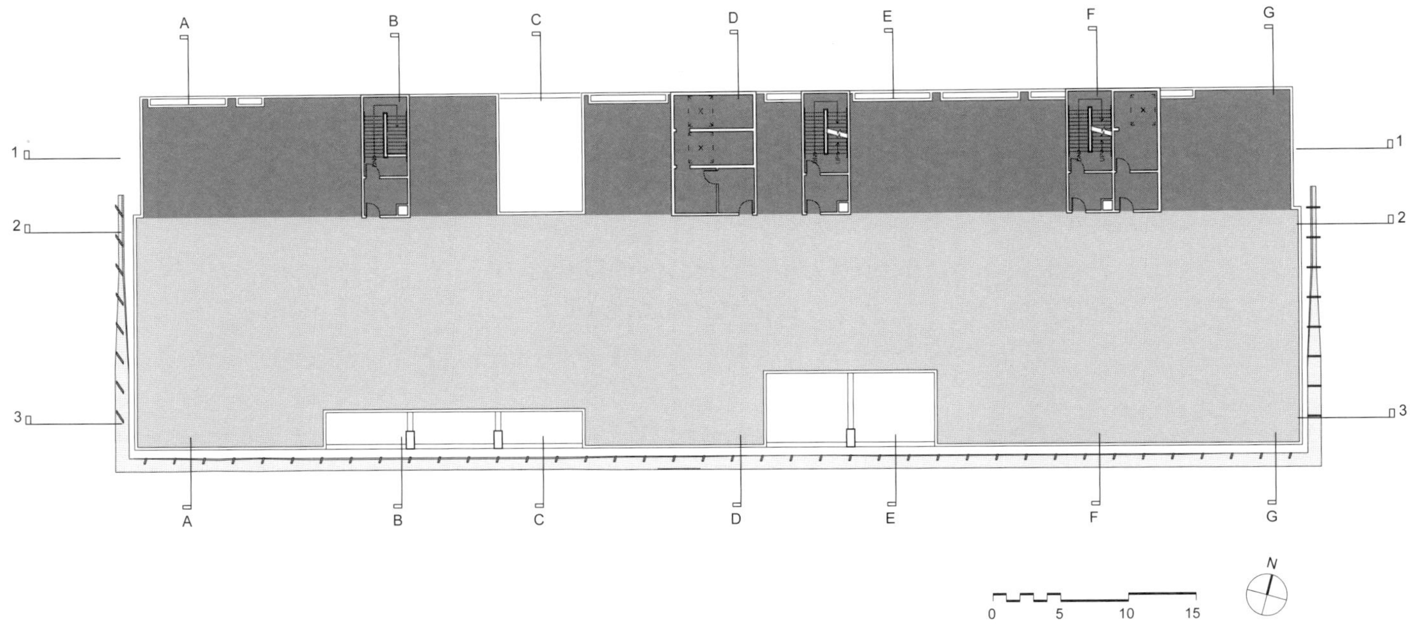

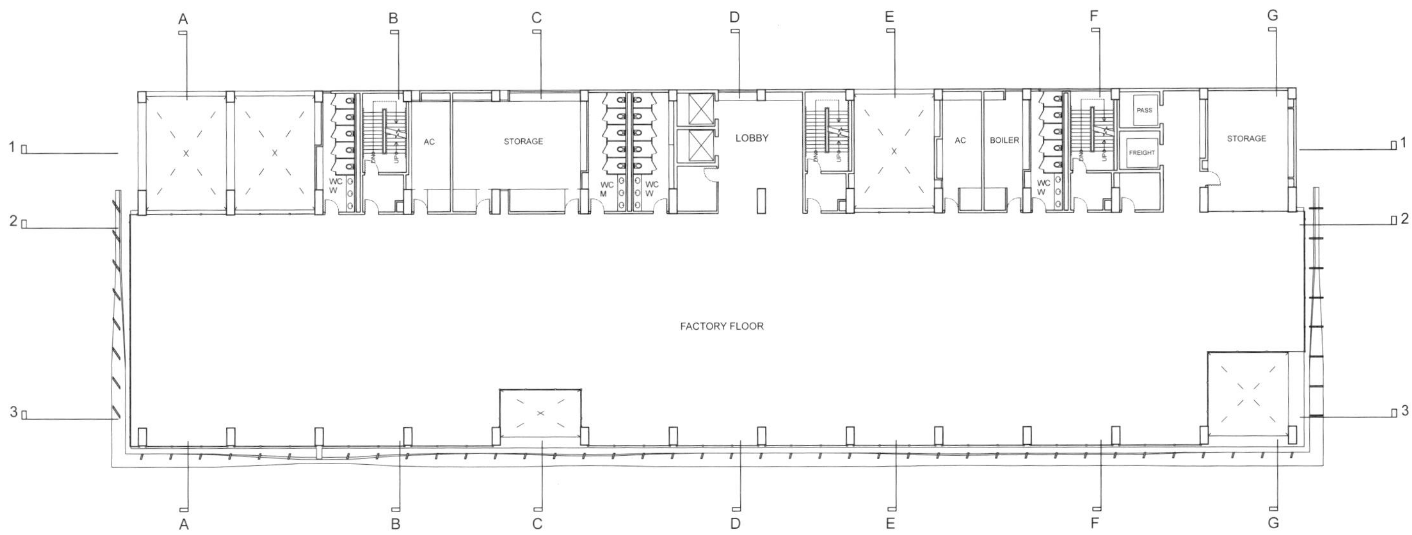

5, 6_ Roof and typical floor plans

Each of the openings begins on one side of the building, carving vertically and horizontally to connect two opposing sides of the building and the factory floors to the sky. In this meandering outdoor carved space, we were careful to produce spatial types that were incongruent with the repetitive, structural bays of the building, longitudinally, transversally, and vertically. In this manner, we believe we were able to create a tension between the repetitive bays of the factory setting and the spatial maneuvers of the carvings. The two work together, but belong to different sets of concerns. One is the result of the absolute structural organization of the building with repetitive elements, and the other is the result of spatial plays, environmental concerns, and plastic moves.

Finally, with collaboration from our Chinese counterparts and their structural engineers, we were able to produce a seismic solution that did not involve breaking the building into three pieces. We, nonetheless, maintained the carvings, due to their spatial, lighting, and ventilation advantages. The building, in its final form, is woven longitudinally, transversally, and vertically with post-tensioned cables. In essence, the seismic solution was to "weave" the entire building together three-dimensionally, and keep it under tension in all three axes.

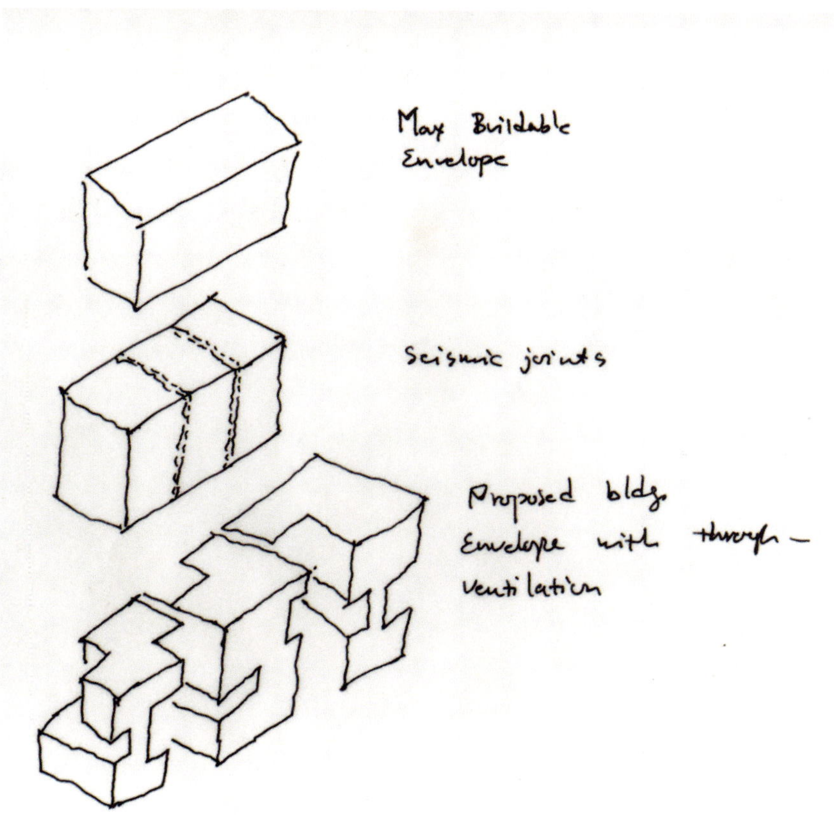

7, 8, 9_ Model images and diagrams
of seismic studies and carvings

10_ Model images
of the carvings

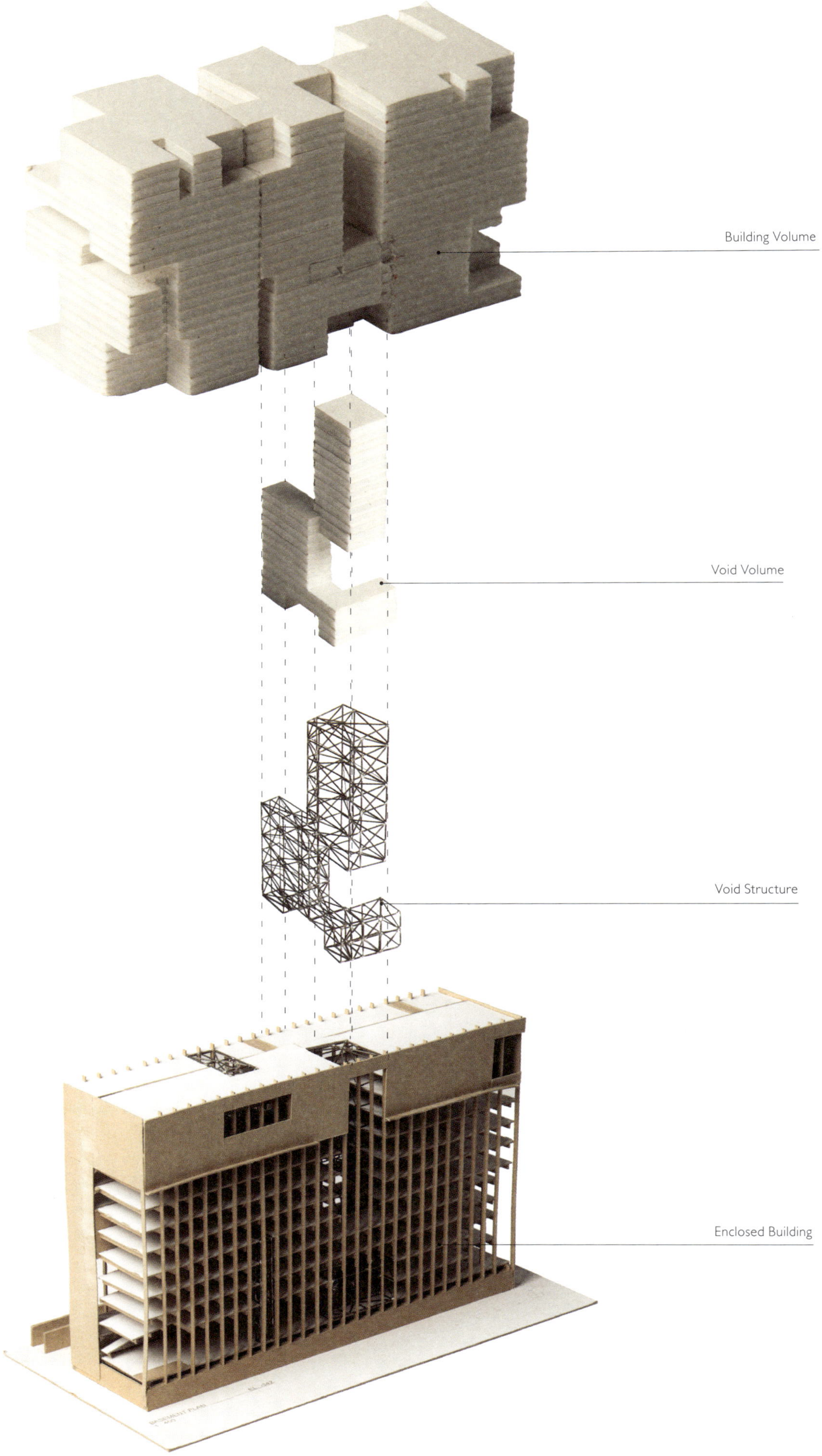

11, 12_ Model images
of the carvings

13_ Environmental diagrams
of the carvings

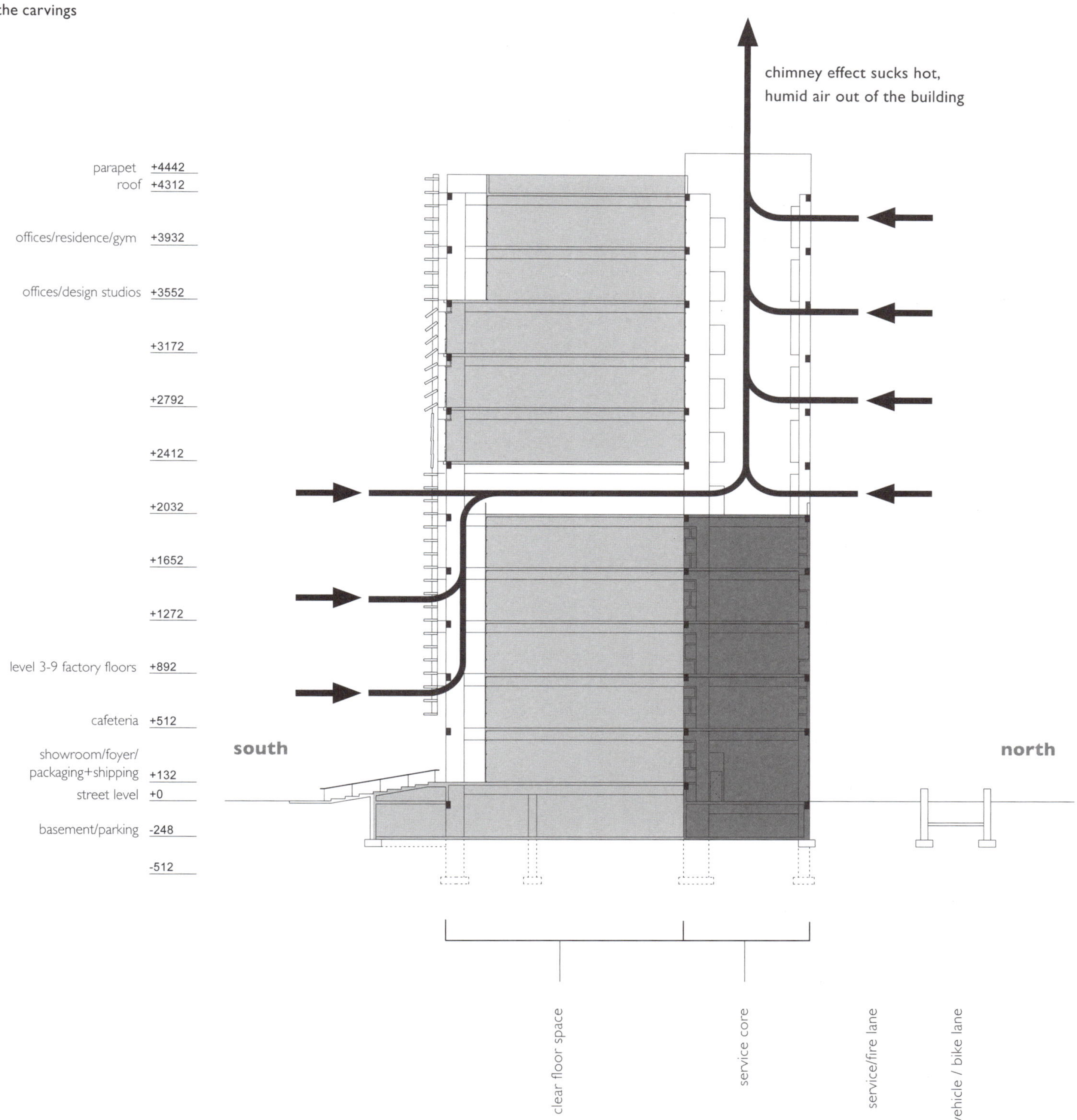

Interlude
Nina Rappaport

L-148 an East/West Vertical Urban Factory

L-148 is a Vertical Urban Factory[1] par excellence in terms of its architectural organization that embraces the typology of a multi-storied factory. Using verticality as a guiding design and production organizational system, the architects have created a project that arises from the modernist typology of the factory as "spectacle," yet is experimenting with sustainability and spatial flexibility. With its unique East/West hybrid outlook in which the Chinese-American owner has built a factory back in his homeland, L-148 has also engaged in progressive workplace measures by spearheading environmental and social well-being as part of its overall corporate philosophy. These directions inspire new values for the future of the global factory reframing the potential for the urban factory to be transparent both in its organization and design as it is reintegrated into the city.

Global Factory

Global trade – with its origins in the earliest days of merchants and vanquishing marauders – increased as advanced technologies, new systems of transport, and expanding economies led to what we now call *globalization*.[2] Over the last century, China with its broad trade networks, became a core trade force through an intensive infrastructure of subcontractor factories that manufactured products for increasing numbers of clients: China as the outsourcer for the world. But, today, as China's middle class grows and the country's leaders adopt capitalism, industrialists in China have turned inward, developing products and a marketplace for their own new middle class, and the new global factory has expanded in countries such as Bangladesh, Cambodia, and Vietnam. Chinese products are not only those that they have copied (which is what they were known for in the last century), but those that they innovate as they had been doing in the first industrial revolution.[3] In contrast to the corrupt practices by some manufacturers – e.g., chemicals stored in violation of environmental regulations, which led to a recent fire in a factory in Tianjin – others have started to follow Western labor standards. With a new consumer increasingly aware of issues of equity in the workplace and sustainable manufacturing, companies now need to shift their focus to social and economic concerns. In addition, many Western companies based in China are beginning to build new factories themselves and have turned their attention to the health and well-being of workers and to creating sustainable workplaces. L-148 is one such example of an East/West hybrid for the vertical urban factory of which we are seeing an increasing number.[4]

The third industrial revolution in China has been dependent on cheap labor for increased profits. Labor is the commodity that Marx defined as flexible because of its potential to change its value more easily than the fixed cost of capital goods, such as equipment and factory real estate.[5] The space in which workers perform their tasks is nevertheless the most neglected of many companies' primary investments. A contract factory (one that does the manufacturing work for others) has little interest in factory design because its needs are standardized; the only requirement is open flexible space that supports production workflow. These factories are usually generic sheds or concrete boxes that house machinery, as a box around technology rather than thoughtful plans that integrate the machines into design and operational programs. In the open-box layouts, the factory can quickly change out the production in order to meet requests from different sources.[6]

Architecturally, these generic sheds, many with pitched roofs for needed height, have roots in an early nineteenth-century typology for large manufacturing sites such as timber and steel work. In the twentieth-century, architect/engineer Julius Kahn, brother of architect Albert

1_ Brinkman & Van der Vlugt, Van Nelle, Rotterdam, 1926–33

Kahn, prefabricated the shed-type factory with the company Truscon Steel with a simple kit-of-parts. During World War II, with the need for fast construction, such manufacturing sheds could be deployed anywhere.[7] Today, these ubiquitous monolithic sheds, air-conditioned and filled with artificial light, conceal the factory operations and thus the workers. Factories, especially in developing countries including China, Bangladesh, Dubai, among others are often sequestered in industrial parks or districts called Export Processing Zones, where the companies receive tax benefits and incentives without any transference of skills or benefits to the local community.[8] In what I call "process removal," factories have been moved outside of cities, to free up urban real estate for "higher and better uses;" factories have even been relocated to the hinterlands, so that city residents no longer see the workers on their daily commute.

The origins of this separation – one that led to many early twentieth century city zoning regulations – was the desire to be separate from pollution and nuisances of factories of the late nineteenth century upon which then numerous American and European early zoning codes were based in the early twentieth century but was further validated by Modern architects and those involved in the *Congrès internationaux d'architecture moderne* (CIAM). Their Charter of Athens, a manifesto of 1933, specified that working and living should be separate.[9] Modern architects, however, didn't imagine the specific design for these industrial districts, or describe the potential relationships between industry and residential uses or the interaction of workers in the city. The land use diagrams were blank as housing was their primary focus and instead they received factory commissions. As the separation of factory from city further widened, it resulted in homogeneous cities oriented towards commercial and residential spaces, rather than manufacturing and the resultant potential jobs.

A Worker's Factory

An alternative to sequestered factories exists, even with the factory owner's focus on profit and control of their workers. Seen in early socialist utopias of architect Claude Nicolas Ledoux for the Royal Salt Works at Arc-en-Senans in France (1775) and continuing with early nineteenth century visionaries such as William Owen in Lanark, Scotland (1801) and Frances Cabot Lowell in Waltham, Massachusetts believed in the positive impact of a better work environment, one that included housing, social services, and schools for workers' children. Some imagined shared profits, others such as Fourier planned buildings such as the *Phalansterie*, which provided living spaces and schools to improve the quality of life in a company town. Jean-Baptiste Andrè Godin actually achieved this goal with a community of four hundred in Guise, France. The town's workers were housed in what he called a *Familistére*, where families lived and the industry was organized in workers' co-operatives.[10]

However, the ideal of a worker's utopia was rarely met because of a company's profit motive, and the industrialist complex became increasingly paternalistic in the early twentieth century as seen with Henry Ford's factory in Detroit (1909); Tomas Bata's factory town in Zlin, Czechoslovakia (1923–32); and even Van der Leeuw's Van Nelle factory in Rotterdam (1926–31). The owner's surveillance of their employees' private and public lives morphed quickly into methods of worker control and became dystopic. Today, the effect of industrialization in China is similar. The migration of farm workers to cities for factory jobs seemingly improves their lives, but yet workers then become dependent upon even low wages in a place, where because of their lack of rights as residents when they are not in their own region, in what is a household registration system called *hukou*, it becomes impossible to get ahead.[11]

Skepticism, because of the profit motive, is called for when a company does provide services to enhance a worker's well-being. In the mid-twentieth century, suburban corporate campuses offered services such as barbershops, post offices, and bowling alleys. Today, companies such as Google and Urban Outfitters offer free meals and entertainment, which entice workers to remain at their jobs longer. This cycle perpetuates similar

2_ Owen Williams, Sainsbury's, London, 1932–33

control mechanisms between the factory owner and their employees that questions the capitalist model. Given this situation, it is important to imagine an alternative to the exploitation of the global factory worker.

The Western Modern Factory

One solution is for more physical and organizational transparency that also benefits the city by using local resources, labor, and commerce. This can be embodied in the vertical urban factory as both an architectural type and as a metaphor for urban industry in general. The result can be true amenities such as better schools, more worker training facilities, and increased employment opportunities. It also reinforces the idea of local industry and goods in global trade or what is often called *glocal*, where things are made locally to be sold both locally and internationally. The Vertical Urban Factory includes two categories: the *layered* factory, which is a often a speculative building, occupied by one or more factories that might use one or more floors. The other type is an *integrated* factory, where one company occupies the entire building for all of its functions – offices, manufacturing, storage, distribution, and more recently, sales.

The manufacturing process can flow from top to bottom, or bottom to top, at first with mechanisms such as chutes, balconies, pulleys, and, later with elevators to increase the efficacy of production flow.[12] The integrated factory also allows companies to see value in design supporting their brand; this occurs most often in what I have referred to as the "spectacle" factory, after Guy Debord, who viewed society, along with its cities, through the lens of commercialization.[13] Taking his term literally, the design of the factory becomes a marketing tool to entice consumers and investors in the same way that a corporate office becomes a showpiece for the client.

One significant aspect, often overlooked, which heightens the potential for experimentation in a factory's design, is the dialogue between the client and the factory owner. When the client and the architect work in close collaboration, the outcome can be transcendent, as seen in Behren's relationship with AEG; his design of industrial objects for the electric company led to his commission for a series of buildings for the company including the renown 1909 Turbine Hall commission and was part of the philosophy of the Werkbund, an association of artists and industrial designers. When Gropius designed Faguswerk in 1913, the company created their identity through both architecture and graphic design anticipating the later Bauhaus pedagogy.[14] Both of the companies believed in "good business is linked to good design" philosophy, ideas which further transpired to be absorbed by corporate culture.

The factory typology also fascinated Modernist architects such as Walter Gropius, Erich Mendelsohn, and Le Corbusier. The factory was the epitome of Modernism, both for the new technologies of mass production within the factory and the experimental capacity of avant-garde building design which used new materials of steel, glass, and reinforced concrete.[15] The Van Nelle factory, designed by Brinkman & Van der Vlugt in 1926–33 **(Figure 1, opposite page),** in Rotterdam

3

4

5

6

3_ Usine Claude & Duval, Le Corbusier, St. Die des Vosges, France, 1947-51

4_ Brise-soleil, Usine Claude & Duval, Le Corbusier, St. Die des Vosges, France, 1947-51

5_ Vertical Urban Factory in Hong Kong

6_ Kowloon Walled City, Hong Kong

exemplified the modern concepts of streamlined production that the owner, Kees van der Leeuw, established for the making of tea, coffee, and cigarettes. A theosophist, Van der Leeuw believed in organizing a comfortable workplace that was hygienic and filled with light and air, exemplified in the glass façade. The production process flowed from top to bottom, with the raw materials delivered to the workspaces above and the finished product transferring on overhead conveyors through sky bridges to the warehouses below. Because the owner of the company directed the construction, there were opportunities for design experiments and programmatic amenities such as a playing fields, cafeteria, glazed stair towers, and a rooftop circular tea-tasting room for clients. Even if the working conditions did not live up to all that Van der Leeuw assumed they would be, the worker was attended to.

Sainsbury's, **(Figure 2, page 55),** the first supermarket chain in Great Britain, and the first poured-in-place concrete building in London, was designed by engineer Owen Williams in 1932–33, after he designed the more well-known Boots factory in Nottinghamshire of 1931 and was touted as a feat of construction.[16] The production in the six-story processing plant for prepared meat dishes also flowed top to bottom, with the offices on the top floor and the workers completing their tasks of sausage-making and pie baking in open, clean, and well-lit spaces below. Its holistic design allowed for efficient movement of goods and the essential food produced there could reach the urban consumer quickly justifying the need for food manufacturing in cities, still today.

Another inspirational modern factory, rebuilt after the destruction of the original factory in World War II, is Le Corbusier's Usine Claude et Duval **(Figure 3),** a five-story undergarment factory in St. Dié-des-Vosges. The owner, Jean-Jacques Duval, acknowledged the workers' needs for light and air. The new factory was situated adjacent to a series of surviving saw tooth shed structures; a gate leads to the new building through a sheltered space for bike parking, formed by the lifting of the building above the ground plane on concrete *pilotis*. Le Corbusier maintained the stone wall at one end of the site, building a compact volume for the factory. He placed the offices on the top floor with an internal circular metal stair connecting to the manufacturing floor, where double-height spaces allow for ample light and air to enter the workspace. A grid of thin concrete *brise-soleil* shields the wood-frame windows from direct sunlight that animates the façade. **(Figure 4, opposite page)** The building's vibrancy is further enhanced with brightly painted elements signifying the various building circulation functions in deep red, yellow, blue, and green. In the efficient circulation of goods and workers – the building functioning literally as a machine.

Eastern Vertical Urban Factories

In China, the vertical urban factory has its vernacular roots in Hong Kong, with its very particular sectional topography. This dense city necessitated that factories be built in multi-stories because of lack of land available for the growing industrial base. In the 1960s, the government supported the construction of what they call "flatted factories" as the layered manufacturing typology, which they leased to different companies in five- to ten-story concrete buildings. **(Figure 5, opposite page)** A second phase of taller factories (up to twenty stories) was built in the 1970s.[17] While many of these factories were demolished when manufacturing moved to mainland China, other manufacturers continue urban manufacturing in the large-scale industrial estates. Building infrastructure and services – as well as the various open and close relationship to the street for loading and access – were privileged over innovative design concepts. Informal manufacturing spaces were also developed in areas such as the now demolished Kowloon Walled City, where in the nooks and crannies of the maze of residential and community spaces, people made goods for sale within and beyond the region. **(Figure 6, opposite page)** In contrast, L-148 in terms of its urban location, the integration of material and worker flow, its multistoried design, the environmental features, and the amenities provided to the community sets a new aspiration for Chinese factory design and factory design in general.

L-148

Lafayette148, a high-end women's clothing company, was started in 1996 by Mr. and Mrs. Siu with their partner Deidre Quinn in New York City's Chinatown. Previously, they operated a garment manufacturing company that made clothes for other fashion designers in the city, including those for which Quinn had previously worked as production manager. The Sius decided to begin their own fashion line and production company in their eleven-story building at the edge of SoHo and Chinatown, and named it after their address, 148 Lafayette Street. Their rent was cheap and, as Quinn noted, "we could make small lots of clothes between the big lots."

Thousands of Chinese immigrant seamstresses worked in downtown factories from the 1960s through the early 2000s, when a combination of events – such as September 11, 2001, and the increased movement of low-cost, mass-produced manufacturing to China and Mexico – reduced the availability of local employment. Added to this was the gentrification of downtown making it more difficult for workers to live close to their place of employment. Lafayette 148 was also affected and sought additional workers in China, first in Hong Kong and then in Siu's hometown of Shantou, China in the Guangdong Province.[18] The city is a one-hour flight from Hong Kong, and has a special economic zone where companies primarily make toys and garments – it is not a large, floating manufacturing center, but, instead, each region has its specialty."[19]

7_ Lafayette 148, worker's craft

8

9

8_ Exterior of building in urban context

9_ Interior manufacturing space

Siu looked to produce more clothes. He started by using seamstresses in Hong Kong, but in May 2002 decided to hire some workers in Shantou. At first there were only three sewers and a cutter, working out of a hotel room. When Quinn went to visit them, Siu asked her what she thought of the factory. Quinn couldn't quite bring herself to call it a "factory." But the following year they found 10,000 square feet of space to house one hundred seamstresses and tailors. At the time, there was still a close worker network that shared skills. Mr. Siu would give cutting lessons to other factories that wanted to learn Lafayette 148's way of working. A leather factory would help Lafayette 148 with the details work and they reached out to the rural network for seamstresses to make special embellishments with beads and sequins at home, in more traditional cottage industries. **(Figure 7, page 57)** Just a few years later, the company expanded and they employed two hundred sewers in a 20,000-square-foot factory. Siu didn't think that the local concrete frame buildings were seismically safe for the extent of production space that he needed. Therefore, he found an empty lot, bought it, and began the process of building his own factory.

Siu envisioned his factory to have more progressive labor conditions than those found in the current factories of mass-produced globalization and he also wanted a building that would represent the design quality of their fashion line as a brand factory rather than a generic global shed. The architects presented three different architectural models and Siu selected the design for a multistoried factory that was the same eleven stories as the New York factory, a kind of mirror of the company. The selected scheme, at 240,000 square feet, was a post-tension concrete frame system, which could provide open floor space that Siu desired as a way to increase flexibility for the machinery layouts. The architects worked with local architects, Shantou Building Consortium, and skilled concrete workers to complete the building. The architects worked with these local contractors in a similar way as Siu worked with factory workers combining the Eastern workforce and Western designers. **(Figure 8)**

L-148 a Renewed Modernist Factory

L-148 – as a vertical urban factory – has roots in numerous modern factories, integrating both form and function, and serve as design experiments, embracing the company's identity. The factory as a space of design exploration is renewed again in L-148 in terms of the material experimentation, structure, urban siting, and the flow of processes within the building. Since L-148 built the factory that it was to own, rather than occupy a building owned by a developer, the organization of the space could be a completely integrated system – from design to production to distribution similar to the Duval, Van Nelle, and Sainsbury's factories.

L-148 has three entrances: workers enter on the north; visitors on the south; and there is a separate, entrance for a showroom. The top two floors house the offices and design studios. The production flow begins at the top with the design and patternmaking, then cutting and sewing and the final garment progresses downwards through nine floors with floors three through nine containing the open manufacturing spaces in which there is flexibility to experiment with new production methods, and to reconfigure the worktables and sewing machines. Long tables line the factory floor in parallel rows, with carts that move from place to place to drop fabric at a sewer's table or to pick up finished goods. What was designed as a double-height showroom is currently a design room for the interaction between designers and sewers similar to that at Duval, which reinforces a fluidity of worker and goods movement. The shipping and packaging occurs on the east side of the building. (**Figure 9**) The company is also focused on sustainability from the building construction method and internal environment to the way they make their products. Sustainability is also a characteristic of the vertical urban factory's potential. By building taller factories in cities, open land is saved, fuel used for commuting is reduced, and shipping energy is kept low.

L-148 also harnesses natural breezes for fresh air and the sun to power the building. The inventive perforated concrete fins on the south side shield the building and workspaces from direct sunlight and the windows draw in air. The holes in the concrete save material and lighten the loads but also dematerialize the concrete as though it is a light fabric veil. It stands as a contrast to that of Sainsbury's solid and massive concrete work but could be considered more similar to the more porous façade of Duval in its dynamism and more ecological orientation with its fins like Le Corbusier's brise-soleil with plenty of light and air. Voids cut into the north façade bring light into the interior and create balconies. An internal vertical void, as a chimney, allows hot air to rise on a north-south axis, then moves up and out to provide cross ventilation, creating a passive cooling system that greatly reduces both the temperature and the humidity in the manufacturing spaces. The energy-cost reduction is also significant: the building uses forty percent less energy for cooling, and has enough energy to continue operations during the city's regular and inconvenient blackouts. In terms of sustainable production, L-148 recycles hangers and plastic bags; they use fabric mills that offer more natural fabrics, and they don't add extra buttons to the garments, as no one ever seems to use them.[20]

Quinn emphasizes both the company's investment in their workers and in their technologies as a synergy that is not exclusive of one or the other. She believes that the company instills pride in the workplace because they all work for one company and they care about what they are making (as much as they can, as the products are still unaffordable to them). This is in contrast to a contract factory, where often workers who work on parts of a product don't know what the finished product will be. Quinn says, "it is not the factory versus the brand; it is a family."[21] They train the workers to make quality products, and promote them up through the various levels of expertise, resulting in a high retention rate of twenty years. But they also invest in the most up-to-date equipment, such as automated laser-cutting machines that can operate 24/7. Sometimes each machine has a different garment in process, which might not be as efficient as mass production, but is a method employed to meet the superior quality of the brand. This also allows the company to react quickly to new order requests and to provide services that contract factories can't because they are making another companies' products.

Similar to the social amenities of the modernist factories, L-148 has engaged in progressive issues by spearheading the workers' well-being and education as part of the company's overall philosophy as in the early days of the Van Nelle factory or even looking to the ideal of the utopian thinkers of the nineteenth century. The workers are paid comparably to other factories in China, where now there is competition for the best workers. The factory itself is also organized in smaller teams – as in cellular manufacturing – so that each worker can often complete a full product from start to finish. They also have health insurance and vouchers for lunch. The Sius decided to start

10_ Fine handwork at Lafayette 148

11, 12_ School of Dreams

a school after they visited a non-English-speaking workers' children's school at holiday time. When they arrived, Siu was shocked that the facilities at the school were in disrepair and that the students needed desks. Then they were told that the school was closing; Siu wanted to start one to help the residents of the city. They rented the building, painted it, and started with one grade, each year it added a grade and now is up to 350 students ranging from kindergarten to sixth grade.[22] This "School of Dreams" was founded for the children of migrant workers within this extended community – not only for the employees' children, who make up only six to seven percent of those enrolled. **(Figures 11, 12)** Many return to their hometown for seventh grade, while others can attend a magnet school for higher grades. Each year the company raises funds for the schools from sample sales in New York. The idea of doing good contributes to the company ethos; the act of giving back to the community then becomes part of their brand.

East/West Intersections

L-148 inhabits an interesting intersection between the East and the West. The company's design team travels to China from Italy and New York City for meetings, to develop the collection, and to work on the unique material combinations such as knitwear with leather or woven fabrics. **(Figure 10, page 59)** Just as in recent automotive plants, design and production are in proximity so that the designers work on the factory floor with the seamstresses, experimenting with new concepts. The factory has pattern rooms in both China and New York so that while one city is sleeping, the other is working, keeping the operations going around the clock.

In general, a company's production cycle is not complete until the goods are shipped to the retail stores. L-148 has new thriving retail spaces in China. But the majority of their products are shipped to New York for wider U.S. and European distribution. To ease this transit system, Mr. Siu invented a steel container in which garments are hung rather than folded. The box slides into the factory elevator and from there is moved out onto a truck and to an airplane. When it arrives at JFK Airport, it is off-loaded and shipped by truck to the Brooklyn Army Terminal. There, they disassemble the paneled container walls, remove them, and roll out the garment racks to the warehouse, from which they are then easily transferable to department stores. The metal panels are then recycled for further use. The container's compactness and invention is on par with that of the clothing design and the factory itself: efficient and well designed.

Furthermore in an interesting East/West twist, in the original L-148 eleven-story building in New York City, not only do they complete the product marketing, design the clothing, make the samples, complete alterations, and have a flagship store – they also have a small factory.

What is actually made in that factory are clothes to export to China, because "Made in the USA" is now a sought after label, completing the full circle of global commerce. L-148 both as a company and as a new paradigm for vertical urban factories combines ideas of sustainability, with that of experimental design, and social needs for renewed urban economies as the bands of twisted concrete both provide shading that mimics fabric folds, representing and supporting the company's identity whose own focus is on quality design and manufacturing in cities.

1 See Nina Rappaport, *Vertical Urban Factory*, (Barcelona: Actar Publishers, 2015).

2 The wider use of the term *globalization* is described in Theodore Leavitt, "The Globalization of the Market," *Harvard Business Review,* May/June 1984, 2-102.

3 Regina M. Abrami, William C. Kirby, and F. Warren McFarlan, "Why China Can't Innovate," *Harvard Business Review,* March 2014.

4 See examples in Nina Rappaport, *Vertical Urban Factory* Actar, 2015, including, VW Dresden, Nord Building in Zurich among others.

5 Karl Marx, Federick Engels, Editor, *Capital* (New York: The Modern Library, 1906): 405-585 describes the various capital investments in a factory.

6 Discussed in Paul Midler, *Poorly Made in China,* (Hoboken, N.J.: John Wiley & Sons, Inc., 2009).

7 Albert Kahn is the more known of the brothers for his work on numerous factories for the automotive industry, particularly Ford in Highland Park in 1909. The repetitive factory typology allowed him to run his own architectural firm like a business and perpetuated the shed-type factory based on the need for the quickly built factories during World War II. His brother Julius was more of an inventor who developed the shed as a product.

8 For further information see: Naomi Klein, *No Logo,* (New York: Picador 1999) and Andrew Ross, *Fast Boat to China,* (New York: Vintage Books, 2007): 136-186.

9 See Ulrich Conrad, *Manifestos of Twentieth Century Architecture* (Cambridge, MA: MIT Press, 1970): 137.

10 See Leonardo Benevolo, *The Origins of Modern Town Planning,* (Cambridge, MA: MIT Press, 1971): 39-48.

11 See descriptions of their life in the factories in Leslie T. Chang, *Factory Girls,* (New York: Spiergal & Grau, 2009).

12 See Nina Rappaport, *Vertical Urban Factory*, (Barcelona: Actar, 2015): 116-121.

13 Guy Debord, *The Society of the Spectacle,* (New York: Zone Books, 11995): 25-34. Originally published in French in 1967.

14 See Annemarie Jaeggi, *Fagus,* (New York: Princeton Architectural Press, 2000).

15 Nina Rappaport, *Vertical Urban Factory,* 141-148. And see also Reyner Banham, *A Concrete Atlantis* (Cambridge: MIT Press, 1986).

16 "New Warehouse at Blackfriars for Messrs J. Sainsbury Ltd.," *Architect & Building News,* January 11, 1936, 61-64

17 Barrie Shelton, Justyna Karakeiwicz, Thomas Kvan, *The Making of Hong Kong from Vertical to Volumetric* (New York: Routledge, 2014): 89-93.

18 The city is a one-hour flight from Hong Kong, and has a special economic zone where companies primarily make toys and garments.

19 Discussion with Deidre Quinn, New York, Summer 2015.

20 Ibid.

21 Ibid.

22 Discussion with Tom Hoi, legal counselor for Lafayette148 New York, Summer 2015.

Sculpting

Mehrdad Hadighi

The building is composed of two general segments. The southern section, extending from east to west, holds the factory floors, open, clear, un-interrupted, naturally lit and ventilated. The northern section, also extending from east to west, contains the service core, stairs, elevators, lobbies, bathrooms, mechanical rooms, and all other enclosed spaces. **(Pages 42-46)** In order for the mechanical and electrical systems to travel from the service core to the factory floor, and from floor to floor, we devised a thick, "sculpted wall" that extends the entire length and height of the building and provides a communication wall that connects everything north with everything south, connecting everything between floors, and everything on the same floor longitudinally.

What appears in concept to be logical and sensible was not so. The most logical and efficient spatial location of the sculpted wall was within the zone of the structural system of the building separating the northern service core from the southern factory floors. However, this inhibited both vertical and horizontal movement; every time an air conditioning duct had to cross from one bay to the next, or from one floor to the next, it intersected with a column or a beam. In response, we thickened the wall and addressed this problem through sculpting it. The wall weaves through the structural columns and beams accommodating both the structure and the mechanical systems that it conveys, permitting both horizontal and vertical movement without intersecting with the structural system.

In the composition of the sculpted wall, we devised a similar system to that of the north façade, working with a limited set of variables that could easily be mass-produced. In their combination we were able to introduce the plasticity of form and space through a playful arrangement of the mass-produced elements.
(Figures 1-2, pages 66-67)

In the sculpted wall we were able to house all longitudinal air conditioning lines, electrical lines, fire-suppression lines, steam lines, door openings connecting the north and south sections, and built-in storage systems for the factory that housed everything from beads and yarns to fabric roles and die vats. **(Figure 3, page 68-69 and figures 4-9, pages 70-71)**

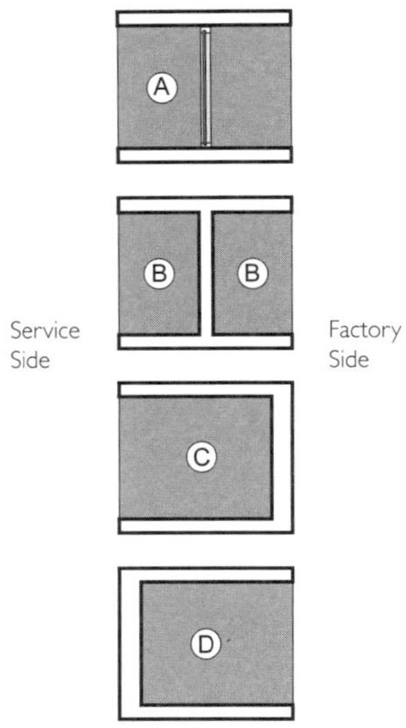

Sectional Key

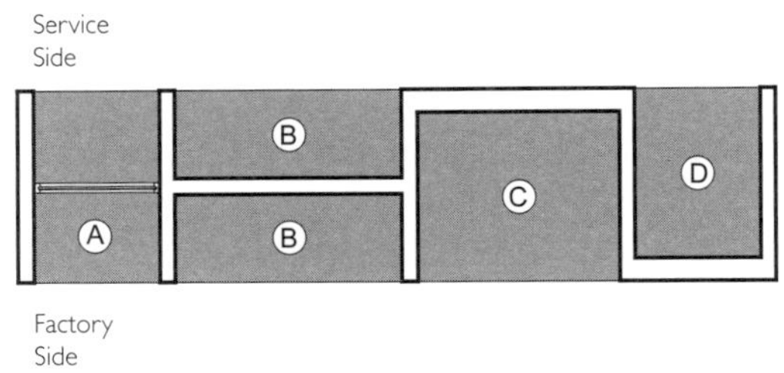

Plan Key

Type A
Thru Wall
Opening W/Window

Type B
Storage for
Factory and Service Sides

Type C
Storage for
Factory Side Only

Type D
Storage for
Service Side Only

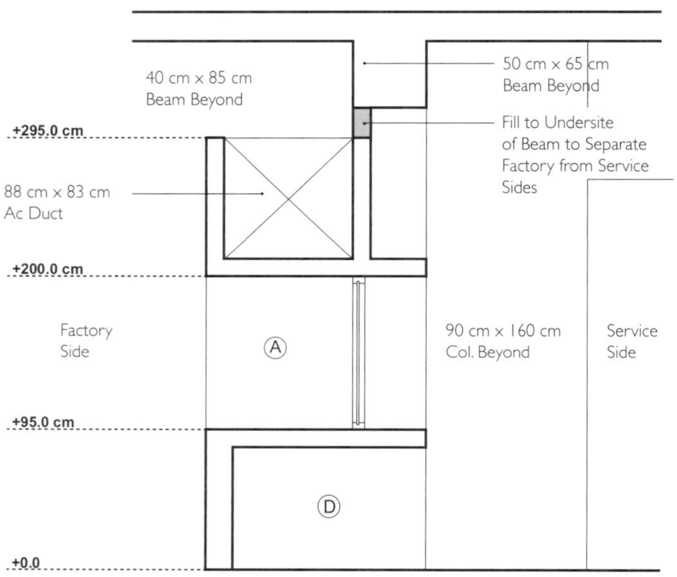

Horizontal
Datum Lines

Sculpted Wall Key

Notes:
Key is for graphic description only. Please reger to dwg.'s
A6 & A602 for typical dimensions and conditions.

Doors
All single doors measure 100 cm W x 200 cm H
All double doors measure 180 cm W x 200 xm H

1_ Plan and section keys of the components
of the sculpted wall

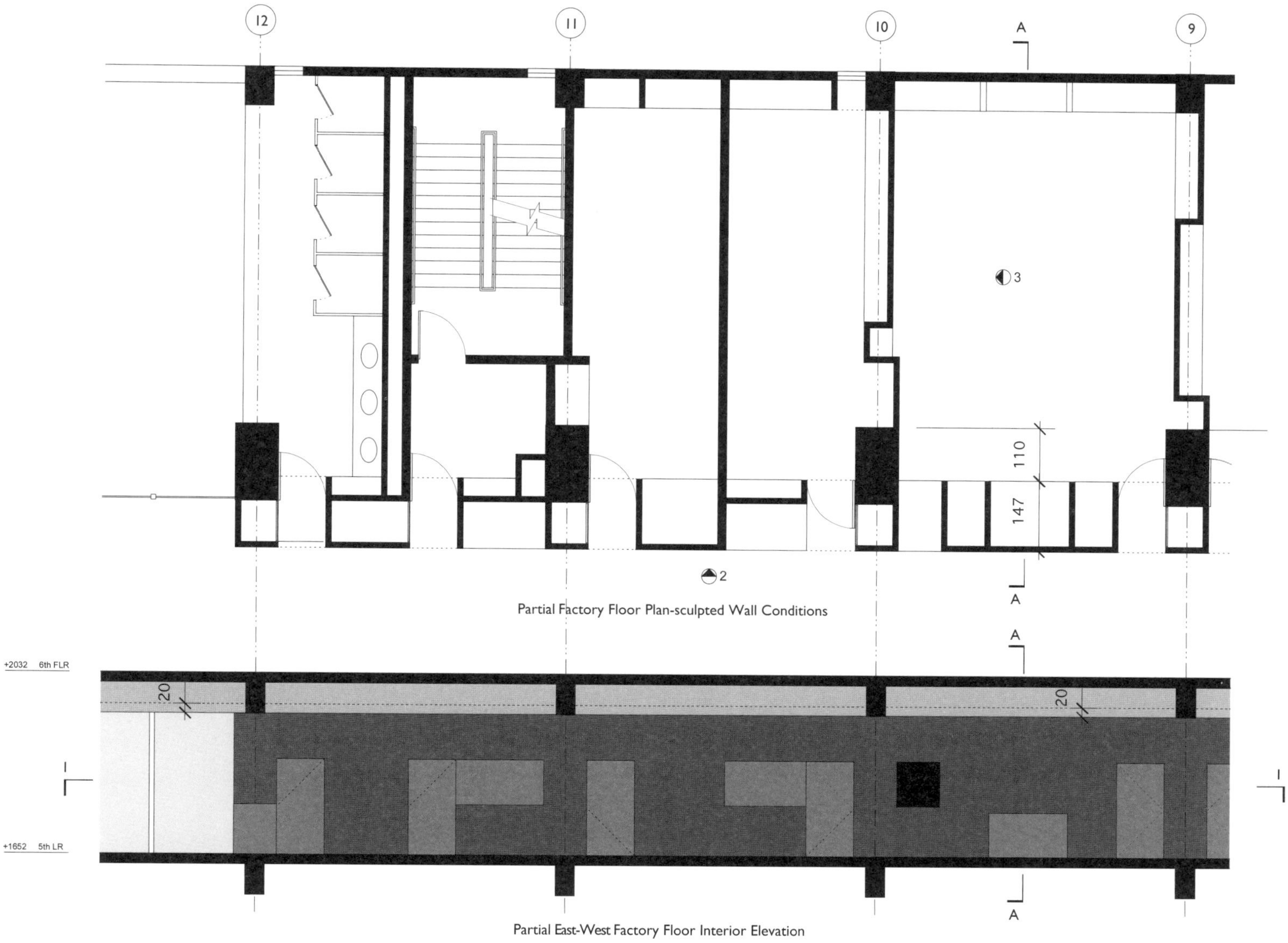

2_ Partial plan and elevation
of the sculpted wall

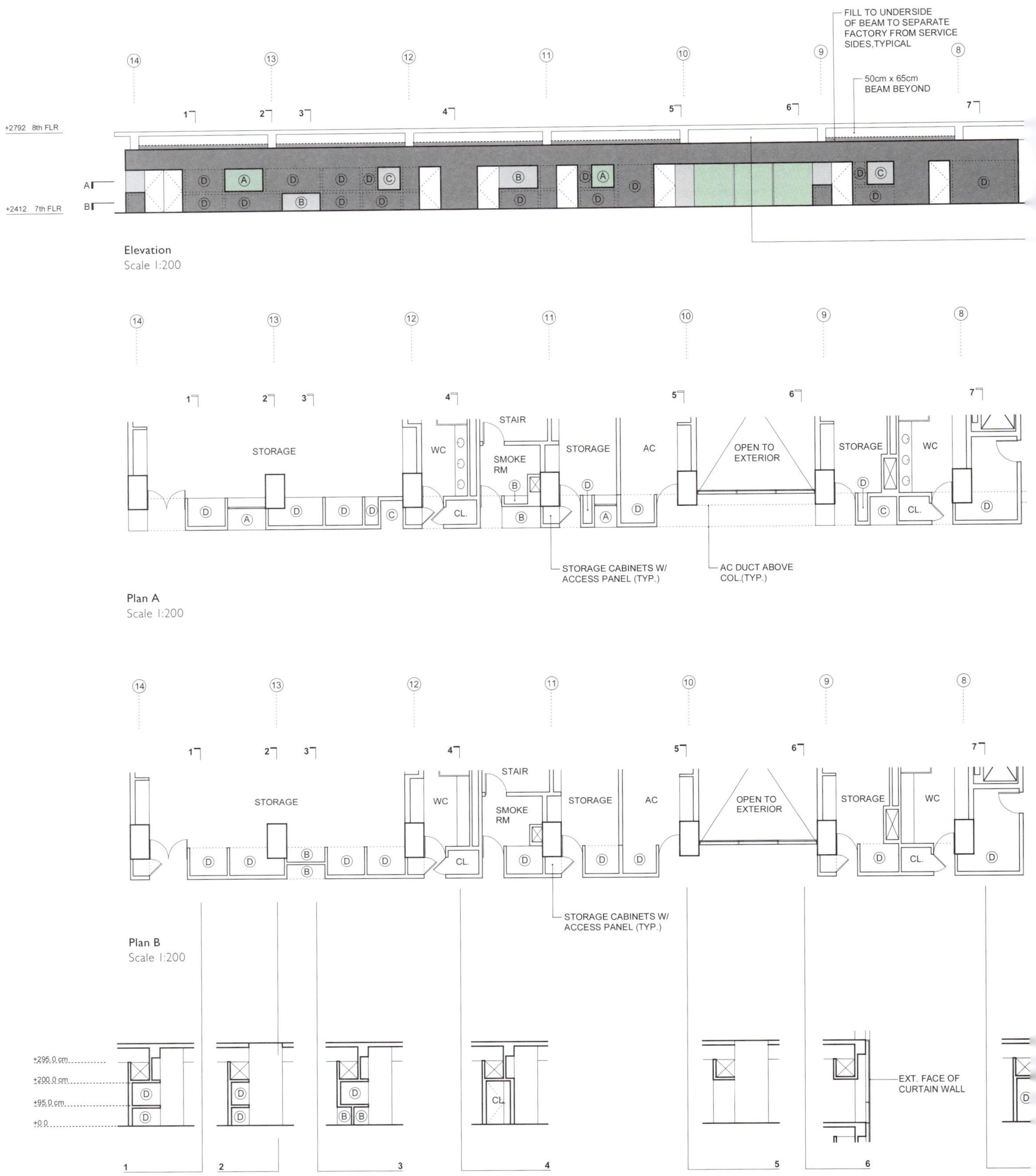

3_ Plans, sections, and elevations of the sculpted wall

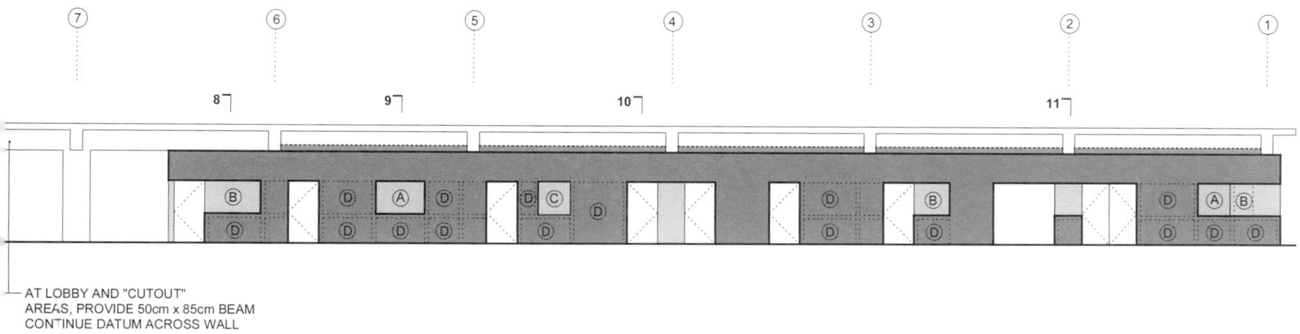
AT LOBBY AND "CUTOUT" AREAS, PROVIDE 50cm x 85cm BEAM CONTINUE DATUM ACROSS WALL

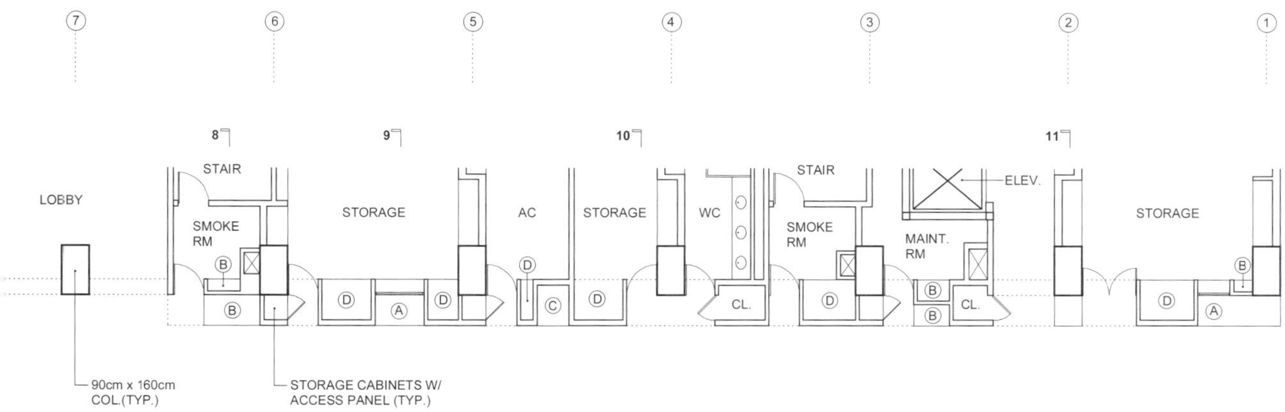
LOBBY
STAIR
SMOKE RM
STORAGE
AC
STORAGE
WC
STAIR
SMOKE RM
ELEV.
MAINT. RM
CL.
CL.
STORAGE
90cm x 160cm COL.(TYP.)
STORAGE CABINETS W/ ACCESS PANEL (TYP.)

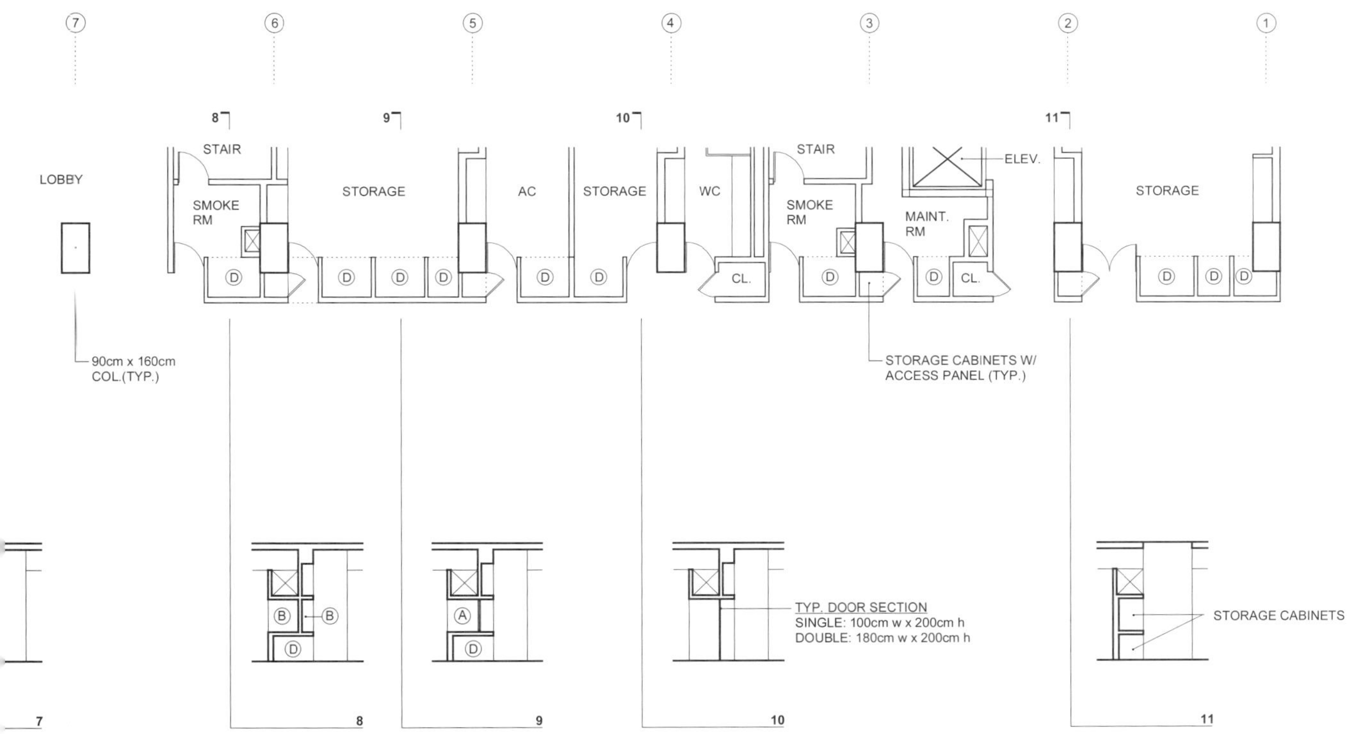
LOBBY
STAIR
SMOKE RM
STORAGE
AC
STORAGE
WC
STAIR
SMOKE RM
ELEV.
MAINT. RM
CL.
CL.
STORAGE
90cm x 160cm COL.(TYP.)
STORAGE CABINETS W/ ACCESS PANEL (TYP.)
TYP. DOOR SECTION
SINGLE: 100cm w x 200cm h
DOUBLE: 180cm w x 200cm h
STORAGE CABINETS
7
8
9
10
11

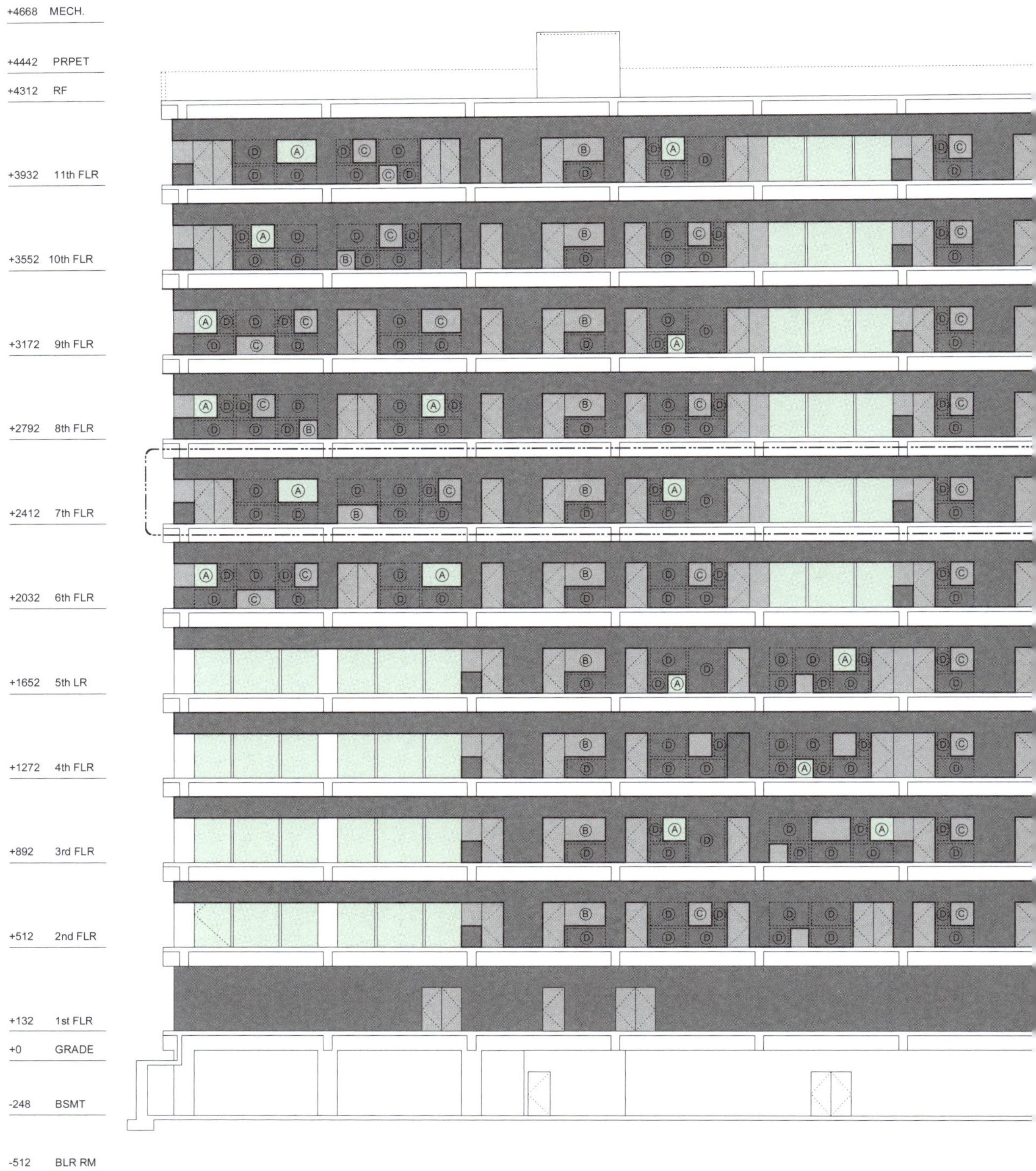

4_ Interior elevation.
Sculpted wall

5-9_ Images of stored items
in the sculpted wall

1
A602

Interlude
Mark Linder

Twisted Image: This is the New Brutal

"... this concept of Image is common to all aspects of The New Brutalism in England, but the manner in which it works out in architectural practice has some surprising twists to it."
Reyner Banham, "The New Brutalism," 1955

I'd like to think that L-148 could be one of the surprising twists Banham had in mind sixty years ago, one that he could not have anticipated of course, but one that he certainly would have recognized. When his now famous article appeared in *Architectural Review*, Banham got The New Brutalism right in principle, even if he never did quite get the story straight. But how could he? In 1955 there really was no story yet to tell. There were only pronouncements, affiliations, a lot of attitude and a few projects that seemed more divergent than similar. But Banham wasn't one for telling it straight anyway, especially if that got in the way of getting it right. His tendency was to mix it up in the moment, to take a position with polemical purpose, to attempt to impact a field still in formation.

All of that is right up front in "The New Brutalism." Banham opens with the provocative question, "What has been the influence of contemporary architectural historians on the history of contemporary architecture?" and follows with a fervent attempt to assert some influence. Going well beyond the claims and statements of The New Brutalism's main protagonists, Alison and Peter Smithson, he calls for "*une architecture autre*"[1] based on two "generalized concepts – image and topology – which, though essentially primitive, have been reached only through immense sophistication."[2] But a decade later, his assessment of himself and The New Brutalism took some surprising twists. In his 1966 book, *The New Brutalism: Ethic or Aesthetic?*, he made clear that he felt his 1955 essay had failed to influence the contemporary field. Still hoping to get it right, but still not quite getting the story straight, he revised his earlier ideas about The New Brutalism and what he saw as the best prospects for modern architecture.

As it worked out, Banham may not have had the influence he hoped for, but that doesn't mean he wasn't right the first time. Today it seems clear that, on this topic at least, Banham was better at contemporary history than past history, especially his own. His 1955 article was one of those rare prognostications that was as audacious as it was prescient. L-148 is the latest evidence that Banham's 1955 insights into post-war, mid-century design culture were not only astute and discerning at the time, but also identified trends and offered explanations that remained, and remain, vital as contemporary possibilities. Even if writing contemporary histories like Banham's are hardly plausible in today's world of the ever-present, a brief time-out to get his ideas straight might show that The New Brutalism is still (and is again) new in L-148, a building that is a powerful instance of, quite literally, the kind of twisted image that he suspected might hold promise for modern architecture. Today, it may be possible – it may be the time to take the time – to make sense of how what he thought then might matter now in new ways.

New or Now?

Banham's theorization of *une architecture autre* as topological "image-making"[3] is increasingly pertinent in today's world of dense, instantaneous, superficial actualities which are as prevalent, and as necessary to grapple with, in architecture's production, reception and dissemination as in any other field. Examples that explore the architectural potential of that reality are wildly diverse, in quality and kind, from Neil Denari to Zaha Hadid to Herzog and De Meuron to James Carpenter to Paul Priessner to Hadigi and Ng. Whether encountered online, in exhibitions or in cities, the surfaces and images of those architectures are the products of, and are calibrated to thrive in, the altered modes of media and exchange that became pervasive after the Second World War and have become immersive today. Banham's claim in 1955, that "basically," The New Brutalism "requires that the building should be an immediately apprehensible visual entity, and that the form grasped by the eye should be confirmed by experience of the building in use,"[4] attempted to reconcile an emerging image-culture, in which anything that circulates as "a coherent and apprehensible visual entity"[5] counts as an artifact, with the fact that those image-entities continue to make their appearances only by virtue of a brute hardware of materials, structures and organizations. That fascination with the effects of technological systems was an enduring theme for Banham. Its implications and potential now are certainly quite unlike what they were in 1955, but the idea remains vital and apt. The environment of magazines, movies and advertisements that intrigued Banham in 1955 must have seemed just as perplexing and astounding to architects then as our computational, networked and globalized systems of social networks and big data does to us now. The economic, social and geo-political shifts that occurred after World War II were hardly more extreme than those that are underway in the early twenty-first century. Banham's attempt to navigate and make sense of that complex time was unapologetically speculative. His aspiration was not to resist the rapidly evolving technologies, economies and cultures of imaging, but to write the contemporary history of what might be called theory and design in the first image age.

Banham continued to champion The New Brutalism for another decade, but his enthusiasm gradually faded as he reconsidered his reasons and revised his estimate of what he called "the immediate future." His commitment to image and topology would never again be as intellectualized, edgy and enthused as it was in "The New Brutalism." His continued writing, and rewriting, of contemporary history led him to other topics, concepts and conclusions, and the differences between his 1955 article and 1966 book must be understood in the context of evolving contemporaneities and new attempts at historical revision. Both were the unstated subtexts of his second, more assiduous and critical attempt to get The New Brutalism right in his 1966 book, which recounts the story of how it was initially developed and promoted in the early 1950s by Alison and Peter Smithson and a few others in Britain, and which assembles an international lineage of its offspring and dispersion over the next decade. Banham diligently reassembles the facts, texts and projects of the beginnings of The New Brutalism in a way that was not possible ten years earlier, but he makes a brilliant muddle not only of how it had worked out in practice in England and beyond, but also of the radical theoretical speculations on The New Brutalism that he had gotten so brilliantly right in the midst of the real muddle of its beginnings.

Banham's 1966 account takes his thoughts on *une architecture autre* in new directions, and treats image and topology as if they were generic, benign architectural concepts rather than the fuzzy, subversive and challenging ideas they had been in 1955. He confesses that he got his contemporary history wrong in 1955, and explicitly dismisses his earlier article as an "attempt to father some of my own pet notions on the movement" which were "not representative of the state of the [New] Brutalist movement at that important time in its evolution."[6] Preoccupied as he was with contemporary history (the missing modifier "new" is perhaps symptomatic), and confident he had it right the second time, Banham was no longer interested in, or had forgotten, why those pet notions once had seemed so compelling and auspicious. In 1966 he was telling the end of a story that he believed had not fulfilled the promise of his earlier ideas, and he was willing to let them pass. He also was distancing himself from the Smithsons, who had developed other ideas of their own, and he was willing to let them pass too. But for architects as historically savvy, intellectually contrarian and divergent in their approach and interests as the Smithsons, it is crucial to revisit the possible sources for their sensibility and attitudes – as well as Banham's – in order to make sense of The New Brutalism and the still latent potential of its aspirations. I think Banham nearly got it right the first time, in real time, and those theories had, and still have, more currency than he acknowledged in 1966, or wanted others to remember. At the very least, his 1966 humility about his 1955 ideas was false and his circumspection was half-hearted: earlier in the book he confidently revived and revised some of those very pet notions to make clear what he still thought The New Brutalism could have been and what he still hoped modern architecture might become. In fact, he already was putting distance between himself and the Smithsons in 1955: that was the actual reason why his pet notions were "not representative … at that important time." Then, as in 1966, he knew he was getting ahead of the Smithsons theoretically, or perhaps it would be more accurate to say, getting ahead of them historically. Banham was disappointed in 1966 not because he had gotten it wrong in 1955 but because the Smithsons and others had not followed his lead.

New or Newer

Banham presents two versions of The New Brutalism's contemporary history in his 1955 article: the first, tamer version was indeed "representative of the … movement at that time," while the second version offers his wilder speculations which, I think it is fair to say, were representative of its *potential* at that time. The first situates The New Brutalism in the context of recent debates among British architects about their relationship to the legacy of "the classic Modern Movement"[7] as "seen against the background of the recent history of history, and, in particular, the growing sense of the inner history of the Modern Movement itself."[8] That account builds on the Smithsons' public statements and two of their earliest projects, the Hunstanton School (1950-54) and the unbuilt Soho House (1953), which together establish the more or less familiar characteristics – a caricature really – of The New Brutalism that was taken up by others and persisted reductively as, simply, "Brutalism."
(Figures 1, 2)

1, 2_ "New": The Smithsons' Hunstanton School (1950-54) and Soho House (1952) exemplify Banham's "first phase" of the New Brutalism.

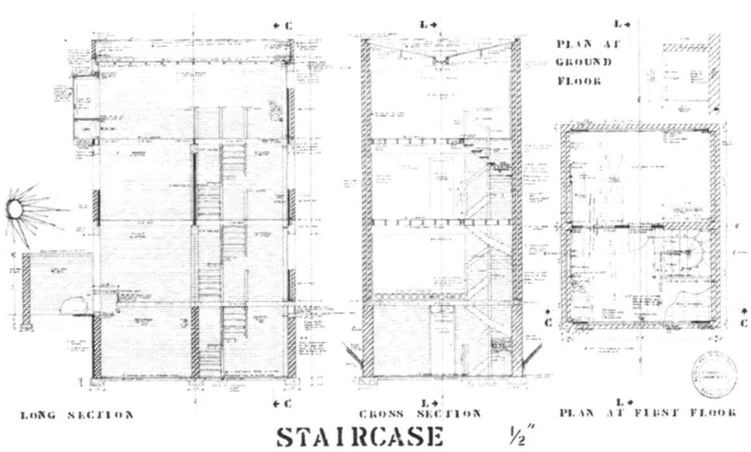

Despite the difference between the steel, glass and brick Miesian idiom of the Hunstanton School and the concrete and masonry "warehouse aesthetic" of the Soho house, Banham offers three intently and earnestly modernist criteria that define those two projects: "formal legibility of plan," "clear exhibition of structure," and "valuation of materials for their inherent qualities 'as found'."[9] But Banham then declares the Hunstanton-Soho "first phase" of New Brutalism too reactionary (a tough-minded intensification of "the basic moral imperatives of the Modern Movement") and too amenable to "crypto-academicism" (a new orthodoxy of formal logics and neo-Palladianism).[10] By 1955, that negative assessment was shared by the Smithsons whose interests and involvements (urbanism with CIAM and mass culture with the Independent Group) were evolving and broadening. But the latter part of "The New Brutalism" launches polemical and theoretical trajectories that are all Banham. He introduces and correlates the concepts of image and topology (as alternatives, in effect, to the current vogue of the picturesque, geometry and proportion) and argues that they are the generative ideas for a newer New Brutalism, and a possible *architecture autre*, that can engage a range of influences, collaborators and audiences beyond architecture.

Banham was riding the wave of his leading role in the Independent Group, as its third and most energetic "convener" from 1952 to 1954. The so-called pet notions in his 1955 article clearly draw on the varied interests in mass media, popular culture, new technologies, and industrial design that were shared by the intellectually adventurous young artists, critics and architects (including the Smithsons), in the Independent Group. Banham's newer version of The New Brutalism was aligned with the Independent Group's interest in "anti-Academic aesthetics" and developments in the arts such as Jackson Pollock' painting, *Art Autre* and *musique concrete* (all of which he would return to in his 1966 book). He even implied that as of 1955 the only built manifestation of the newer New Brutalism was the 1953 exhibition *Parallel of Life and Art*, an all-over installation of enlarged photographic and photographed images from diverse sources (artworks, x-rays, newspapers, magazines, and science) curated by the Smithsons in collaboration with the photographer Nigel Henderson and the sculptor Eduardo Paolozzi. **(Figure 3, page 78)** Two unbuilt architectural projects by the Smithsons also exemplified the newer approach: their competition entries for Golden Lane housing (1952) and the Sheffield University extension (1953) explore the possibility for architecture to "create a coherent visual image by non-formal means, … and [by] fully validating the presence of human beings as part of the total image."[11] **(Figure 4, page 78)** In attempting

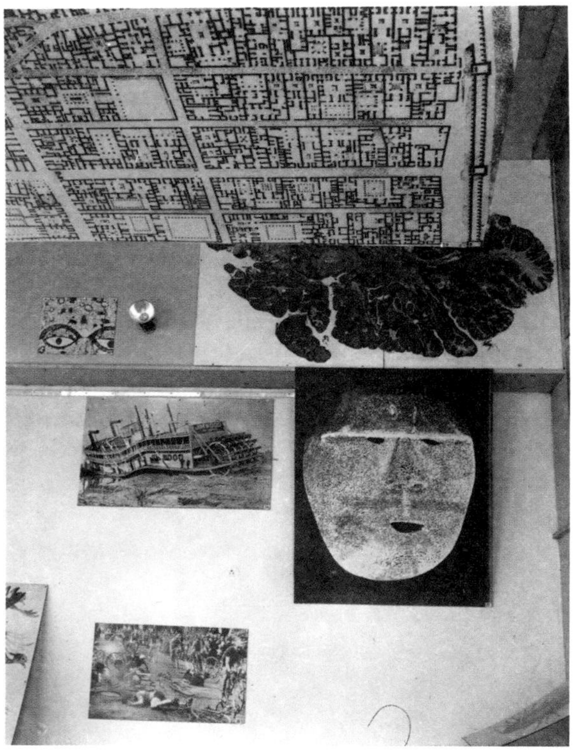

3, 4_ "Newer": According to Banham, the Smithsons' entry for the Golden Lane Housing competition (1952) and the exhibition, *Parallel of Life and Art* (1953), a collaboration by the Smithsons, the sculptor Eduardo Paolozzi and the photogrpaher Nigel Henderson, "enabled Brutalists to define their relationship to the visual world in terms of something other than geometry," namely, "image and topology."

to explain the potential of this approach, Banham gets ahead of the Smithsons, and articulates, though not entirely consistently, definitively or explicitly, a theory of the newer New Brutalism. That theory, and an alternative set of characteristics can be pieced together from three evocative phrases that appear in various places in the article: "memorability as an image," "obsessive emphasis on basic structure," and "abstemious under-designing of details, and... ineloquence."

So while it was Banham's clear intent to distance himself in his 1966 account from the directions the Smithsons and others had taken under the label of The New Brutalism, his differences were already declared in 1955 with his pejorative characterization of a "first phase" which, to Banham's disappointment a decade later, persisted as "Brutalism" and was never succeeded by the "other" approaches he thought were possible. Thus, his position in 1966 is complex, both reviving and refuting his earlier ideas and assessments. He downwardly revised his estimation of the Golden Lane and Sheffield projects, shrugged off the boldest aspects of his own theorization of a newer New Brutalism and reintroduced his idea of *une architecture autre*, making it even more radical and explicit. Most important to understand is that, in 1966, Banham was no longer writing the contemporary history of The New Brutalism because he no longer viewed it as timely. He thought there was only its past history left to write and that his earlier ideas were effectively moot in regard to what had become of The New Brutalism. But it seems he thought those ideas were still applicable in revised form to contemporary trends. He recuperated them in the service of another contemporary history: his new enthusiasms went for Pop, environment, and technology.

Autre New

Banham's augmented idea of *une architecture autre*, which had been only a tentative and undeveloped aspiration in 1955, rejected one of the three basic aspects of The New Brutalism. In 1966 he added structure to geometry as a proscribed "traditional" space-making device: "*une architecture autre* ... ought to abandon the idea that the prime function of the architect is to employ structure to make spaces."[12] His intriguing but not entirely convincing examples of this a-structural direction (unconvincing because his explanation is so cursory) are Buckminster Fuller, for whom "the structure is simply a means toward, the space merely a by-product of, the creation of an environment,"[13] and "a drive-in cinema, where the structure above ground level encloses no space, and the cultural symbols are transient light play."[14] With the latter example, which is illustrated enigmatically by an unidentified high-contrast photograph at the bottom of the page, image and topology return in a new form that suggests a range of possible references and trajectories beyond Pop, from the Eames's installation of their multi-screen film *Glimpses of the USA* in a Fuller dome at the 1959 Moscow World's Fair, to Cedric Price's Fun Palace (1961), to Robert Venturi's Bill-Ding-Board (1967), to John Hejduk's Wall House (1968). **(Figures 5,6)**

What Banham meant by topology and how it relates to structure are crucial, though obscure. Key to the transition from the "first phase" of Brutalism was the abandoning of geometry as it was used in the Hunstanton and Soho projects because, he claimed, it "was only an *ad hoc* device for the realization of 'Images'."[15] Thereafter, "formality" could be "discarded" and topological shapes and surfaces could replace geometric forms as the dominant visual and spatial organizational devices.[16] This was possible, he argued, only after "*Parallel of Life and Art* had enabled Brutalists to define their relationship to the visual world"[17] in "aformal" ways.

By 1966 Banham would expand his understanding of a-formality to include structure as well, essentially dismissing the "obsessive emphasis on basic structure" that was one of his three core aspects of The New Brutalism in 1955, aligned with the move toward image and topology. In 1966, however, he declared that "since the Renaissance"[18] structure was conceptually inextricable from geometry in architecture. This "traditional" association of geometry and structure may have first occurred to Banham less than a year after "The New Brutalism." In his review of *This is Tomorrow*, an exhibition which featured twelve collaborative installations by groups of architects and artists, Banham identified a disappointingly traditional collusion between structure and geometry in most of the projects. As a result, most installations didn't fulfill the ambitions of the show. For Banham, "the most stimulating aspect of the whole exhibition" was its aim "to smash all boundaries between the arts" and to "embrace all the available channels of human perception."[19] But he found the pervasive "technique of category-smashing" disappointingly limited to two channels, amounting in most cases to the construction of what he called "structure-sculptures" in which "some concept of structure – geometry clothed in substance – proved to be the basic, or unifying postulate of most groups' offerings."[20] That critique implicated *Patio and Pavilion*, the project produced by the Smithsons, Henderson, and Paolozzi. Banham took issue with the Smithsons' simple rectilinear shed and enclosure (as well as the images and objects positioned in the space by Paolozzi and Henderson) because they "showed the New Brutalists at their most submissive to traditional values."

Banham saw the Smithsons' version of structure-sculpture in the same way he saw their expressed aim to "represent the fundamental necessities of the human habitat."[21] Both were, "in an exalted sense, a confirmation of accepted values and

5, 6_ "Autre New": Revising his ideas on New Brutalism in 1966, Banham proposed that *une architecture autre* should "abandon the idea that the prime function of the architect is to employ structure to make spaces" and should instead emulate "environments" like "a drive-in cinema, where the structure above ground level encloses no space, and the cultural symbols are transient light play."

5.2 A note on 'une architecture autre'

What is a subversive proposition in architecture – which, as an art, has been forced, by outside circumstance, to absorb many concepts and usages felt to be hostile to its best traditions, and yet has survived? There was something in the air in the middle of the nineteen-fifties that suggested that a really subversive trend was emerging, something that the traditions of architecture could not absorb, and it was to label the intimations of such a trend (discernible in the Smithsons' Sheffield scheme) that the present author coined the term 'une architecture autre' in December 1955. Whatever I thought I meant by the term at the time, it was snapped by Udo Kultermann ('Baukunst und Werkform', August 1958) in an article subtitled 'Ein neugeknüpfter Faden der architektonischen Entwicklung' (A newly-tied thread of architectural development) but he so narrowed the meaning of the term, to cover little beyond the purely formal alternatives to 'rectangular' architecture, that it is necessary here to re-establish the full meaning of the phrase in terms of the New Brutalism.

As has been implied already, the term was coined by analogy with Tapié's concept of 'un art autre', and was intended to stand for something equally radical. That is, an architecture whose vehemence transcended the norms of architectural expression as violently as the paintings of Dubuffet transcended the norms of pictorial art; an architecture whose concepts of order were as far removed from those of 'architectural composition' as those of Pollock were removed from the routines of painterly composition (ie balance, congruence or contrast of forms within a dominant rectangular format – we argued much whether Pollock paid any regard to the edges of the canvas when dribbling his action paintings); an architecture as uninhibited in its response to the nature of materials 'as found', as were the composers of 'musique concrète' in their response to natural sounds 'as recorded'.

Thus, the final and absolute abandonment by 'musique concrète' of any traditional kind of scale or even the twelve-tone series, and with it the abandonment of any kind of harmony or melody (in the sense accepted in the theory of music as taught in the 'conservatoires') gave a measure of the extent to which 'une architecture autre' could be expected to abandon the concepts of composition, symmetry, order, module, proportion, 'literacy in plan, construction and appearance', in the sense accepted in the theory of architecture as taught in the Ecoles des Beaux-Arts, and piously preserved in the Modern Architecture of the International Style and its post-war successors. By this token, 'une architecture autre' ought also to have abandoned even the idea of structure and space – or rather, it ought to abandon the dominance of the idea that the prime function of an architect is to employ structure to make spaces.

Many would agree that to abandon this structure/space synthesis is to abandon architecture altogether, but all that is really abandoned is the notion of the art of architecture that has been current since the Renaissance. Society at large has never shown much interest in this notion, because it has nothing to do with the architect's function in relation to society. What the corporate and private patrons, who have had to represent the desires of society, have demanded of architects is environments for human activities and symbols of society's cultural objectives. For most of human history some kind of space/structure artefact has been the unquestioned manner of satisfying both these desires, but this was never the only possible solution, and it is even less so today. A modern example would be a drive-in cinema, where the structure above ground level encloses no space, and the cultural symbols are transient light-play. But one can adduce much more primitive and genuinely a-formal examples than this, entirely devoid of structural elements or enclosed volume. The camp fire of a nomadic tribe, for instance, creates an environment for human social activity and marks it with a powerful symbol, but the size and shape of the useful environment are defined by no structure, simply by the heat of the fire, the strength and direction of the wind, the physiology of the individuals involved and the activities they are performing.

Given a genuinely functional approach such as this, no cultural preconceptions, and the full battery of modern mechanical services, an 'other architecture' might well employ structure merely as a way of holding up other environmental controls, without endowing it with the monumental significance it enjoyed when massive construction was almost the only environmental control mankind possessed, and with these controls it might or might not happen to define a space without endowing that volume with the cultural significance loaded on it by societies trapped within volumes defined by massive structures.

Formless (sic) buildings, such as Frederick Kiesler's 'Endless House' or Herb Greene's dwelling house

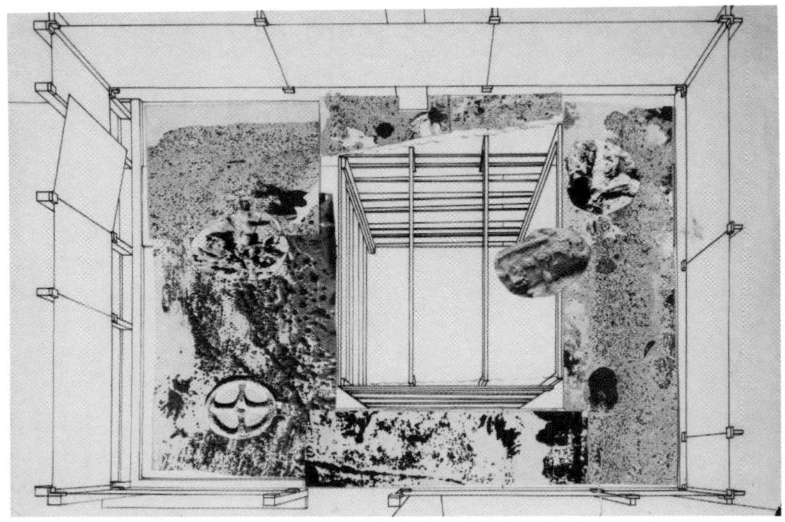

7, 8_ "Concrete Images": In 1956, Banham argued that *Patio and Pavilion*, a second collaboration by the Smithsons, Paolozzi and Henderson, was an architecture that did not rely on "abstract concepts, but on concrete images" to activate its space.

symbols."[22] In that respect, *Patio and Pavilion* was entirely unlike the project in the exhibition that Banham admired most. He was enthralled with the environment of "optical illusions, scale reversions, oblique structures and fragmented images" produced by John Voelker, Richard Hamilton, and John McHale. Its complex confusion of visual modes and information (such as projected movies, billboard images, diagrams, patterns, and even a working jukebox) required the visitor to take "individual responsibility for his own atomized sensory awareness of images of only local and contemporary significance."[23] Yet Banham did not see *Patio and Pavilion* as entirely submissive to traditional values. In the end, he identified a crucial similarity between the two projects that superseded their divergent attitudes toward structure. The Voelker-Hamilton-McHale project, "curiously, seemed to have more in common with the New Brutalists than any other, and the clue to this kinship would appear to lie in the fact that neither relied on abstract concepts, but on concrete images – images that can carry the mass of tradition and association, or the energy of novelty and technology, but resist classification by the geometrical disciplines... ."[24] **(Figures 7, 8)** That last phrase, 'resist classification by the geometrical disciplines,' is the crux. In 1956 Banham understood *Patio and Pavilion* as an environment of concrete images *despite* its concern with "the mass of tradition and association" and its overt use of basic geometry and structure. Its evasion of "geometrical discipline" was partial and sublimated, while the unconventional design of Voelker-Hamilton-McHale fully engaged "the energy of novelty and technology" and resisted the very possibility of being classified as geometric. Thus, in 1956 Banham had a more expansive idea of The New Brutalism that included a broader range of structural attitudes than he would accept ten years later. When he discussed *This is Tomorrow* in his book, he did not mention, or recollect, his earlier claim of a "kinship" between the two projects based on their production of "concrete images." Instead, he characterized them as irreconcilably opposed. In 1966 he saw only the Voelker-Hamilton-McHale project as contemporary, and unaffiliated with The New Brutalism, praising it as "the first Pop-Art manifestation to be seen in any art gallery anywhere in the world."[25] He categorically dismissed *Patio and Pavilion* as "an appeal to fundamentals in architecture [and] an appeal to tradition and the past."[26] Looking back, Banham decided *Patio and Pavilion* was the first indication that the Smithsons had "abandoned their extreme anti-traditionalist position of 1953" and "were withdrawing imperceptibly from their close approach to an Other Architecture."[27] Banham was preoccupied by the simple structure and geometry of *Patio and Pavilion* which recalled the first phase of The New Brutalism as pursued in the Hunstanton School and the Soho house rather than the imaging qualities which he has once found contemporary and compelling. But more important, in 1966 he saw *Patio and Pavilion* as allied with the obsolete logic of architectural structure that he had come to see as a primary impediment to his updated Pop version of *une architecture autre*.

Thus Banham failed to see how both projects could be understood to exemplify the devices and effects of his drive-in cinema. The imaging that Banham had commended previously in *Patio and Pavilion* was not simply an effect of the pavilion and other artifacts in the space. A crucial aspect of the project was how the environment was reflected and multiplied by the aluminum-faced plywood surface of the patio enclosure. **(Figure 9, page 81)** This was the most active feature of the design, producing a complex extension of the surfaces of the pavilion, the contents of the patio, and the circulating visitors. The geometry and structure of the pavilion were indeed extremely basic, but in that way they actually were more like the structure and space of the drive-in than were the multi-media, fun-house tactics of the Voelker-Hamilton-McHale project. The reflective enclosing surface of the patio (which Banham did not mention in 1956 and which in 1966 he saw simply as a use of "non-traditional materials")[28] activated the space in a way that is distinctly aligned with the drive-in's environment produced by the screening of cultural images in an a-structural space.

The Smithsons certainly saw it that way in retrospect. When *Patio and Pavilion* was reconstructed in the late 1980s, they emphasized precisely that aspect of the project in their lectures and in their decision to take photographs that restaged the views that they and Henderson had shot in 1956.[29] Most interesting is that, looking back, they saw distinct affiliations between the spatial and imaging effects of *Patio and Pavilion* and those of Mies's buildings.[30] Their attitudes had come full circle, from taking Mies's Chicago idiom as the inspiration for the first New Brutalist project in 1950 to their reaffirmation of his influence in their lectures and essays from the late 1960s into the 1990s. They were especially fascinated by the Barcelona Pavilion which, like *Patio and Pavilion*, had been reconstructed in the 1980s and seems to have intensified their convictions about the significance of his work. This affirmed Mies as a key figure not only in the history of The New Brutalism, but in the ongoing differences between Banham and Smithsons since the 1950s regarding his work. Banham never saw the kinds of potential and significance in Mies that was expressed by the Smithsons. He always saw Mies as a modernist "master" from whom *une architecture autre* necessarily departed.[31] He never shared the kinds of fascinations the Smithsons found in the Barcelona Pavilion; in fact, in *Theory and Design in the First Machine Age*, Banham identified that project as entirely disengaged from the "technological culture" he endorsed and as exemplary of the "purely symbolic" and "aesthetic" approach of the International Style that he rejected.[32] Yet, what the Smithsons saw in the reconstructed Barcelona Pavilion (and what Banham did not live to see) was conceptually similar to Banham's 1966 proscription against structure as a space-making device. There is a powerful connection between the elements and environment of *Patio and Pavilion* and Mies's polished onyx surfaces. (**Figure 10**) Even more intriguingly, his famous chrome-plated cruciform columns seem to literally explore aspects of Banham's intimations about a new dissociation between structure and space.

In any case, and regardless of the revisions and recollections that complicated his views, it seems Banham's objection to *Patio and Pavilion*, in both 1956 and 1966, was directed less at its basic structure and geometry than at its association (as an artifact and as explained by the Smithsons, Henderson and Paolozzi) with timeless human needs and elemental shelter. It's understandable that as Banham was revising his concept of *une architecture autre*, he came to see *Patio and Pavilion* reductively in terms of his hyperbolic rejection of structure. But he did not have to: he could simply have reiterated his judgement that after the Hunstanton-Soho phase of The New Brutalism, architects needed to reject the criterion of an integrated "relationship between structure, form and function [as] the basic commonplace of all good building."[33] He could have refined and amplified his earlier appeal for architects to seek more radical attitudes toward the relationships between structure and images. In fact, he could have found numerous possibilities to support a more capacious position in none other than Richard Hamilton's early work, such as his 1950 drawing "Structure" and his series of "Trainsition" paintings that followed it. (**Figure 11, page 82**) Hamilton continued to pursue those ideas productively even into the 1970s and 1980s, for example in the peculiar spatial effects produced

9, 10_ "Autre Structure": The reflective enclosing surface of *Patio and Pavilion* has clear affinities with both the drive-in's screening of cultural images in an a-structural space and Miesian surface effects.

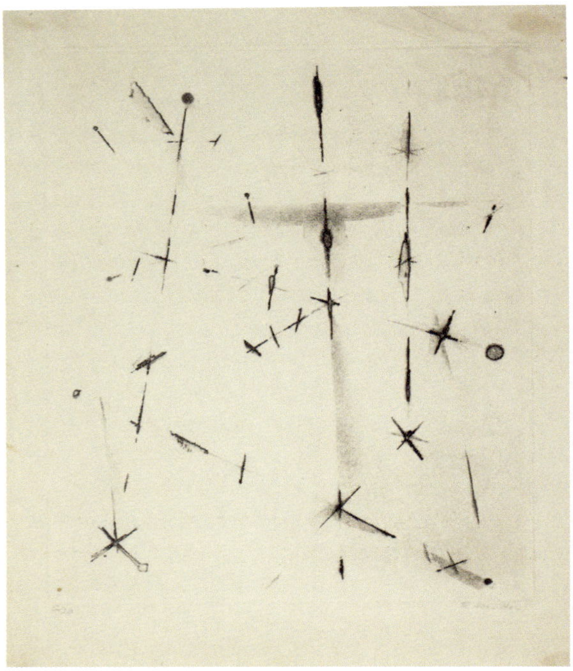

11, 12_ "Autre Autres": Looking back at the Miesian sources of The New Brutalism, and the Smithsons' affiliations with the Independent Group, one can imagine an expanded range of possible convergences between basic structure and *une architecture autre*.

by his diverse models, drawings, installations, paintings, and prints based on a postcard image of the oddly banal lobby of the Hotel Europa in Berlin. I think Banham had it right in 1956 when he saw *Patio and Pavilion* and the Voelker-Hamilton-McHale installations not as opposed, but as occupying different places on The New Brutalist spectrum: together those projects demonstrate a range of possible convergences between basic structure and *une architecture autre*.
(**Figure 12**)

Newer Now

L-148 can be understood as occupying a place on the New Brutalist spectrum close to *Patio and Pavilion*. It may seem overly convoluted to explain a building designed to exploit the constraints of early twenty-first century China by reconsidering a set of ideas and attitudes that were developed sixty years earlier in Britain. But the temporal and conceptual correlations of contemporary history open up compelling and specific affiliations with The New Brutalism. Like the Smithsons' Hunstanton School, their competition entry for Sheffield University or *Patio and Pavilion*, L-148 is an insistently rational yet idiosyncratic and contingent building that produces intensely elusive and uncanny images. Like *Patio and Pavilion*, L-148 recalls the New Brutalist insistence on being both contemporary and rudimentary: it is tempting to consider the ways in which the aspiration of *Patio and Pavilion* to convey an image of dwelling in a culture emerging from a World War is analogous to the ways L-148 engages and reconfigures the design culture, building industry and systems of production in China's new economy. However complex that analogy might be, it is preferable to discussing L-148 in terms of today's current preoccupations with "fundamentals," "object," or "shape." Those simpler contemporary terms and tendencies lack the capacity to pursue the historical, discursive and disciplinary implications of L-148's design. Unlike the vast majority of recent architecture that embraces simplicity and ingenuity, but then adds some whimsy, irony, or cleverness to lighten or enliven its surface, L-148 offers its logic straight, but with a twist. I'd like to think that twisted logic is The New Brutal. L-148, as clearly and compellingly as any recent building, recuperates The New Brutalist preoccupations with the robust versatility of basic modernist sources and principles, the openness and directness of basic structure and raw details, an awareness of history and its place in contemporary history and, most important, the contemporary possibilities of imaging in architecture that Banham identified in 1955. The point is not simply that L-148 should be considered as an addition to the lineage of The New Brutalism; more important, it provokes revisions of that lineage in line with Banham's 1955 speculations, and invites a contemporary version of the kind of contemporary history that Banham practiced, but in terms of some pet notions of my own.

L-148 invites a reconsideration of one of the great confusions of The New Brutalism: how its initial inspiration in Mies van der Rohe's Chicago idiom of steel, glass and brick soon was displaced by a fascination with the *beton brut* of Le Corbusier's *Unite de Habitation*. L-148 is one example of where The New Brutalism might have gone had it not devolved into a Brutalism synonymous with that mode of reinforced concrete construction. Banham's attempt to track that lineage in his book does address that confusion, but his narrative is ultimately dismissive. One of his examples, however, opens especially poignant affiliations to L-148 that should not be dismissed. Banham mentions the building designs of the engineer and "great British anti-aesthete Sir Owen Williams" as the only "conceivable precedent" for the Smithsons' Sheffield project. Banham's attempt to affiliate The New Brutalism with Williams's work is more wily and insightful than his extremely limited observation suggests: "the relationship of structure to glazing may have been remotely suggested by … the 'Dry' manufacturing block [1935-38] (but not the well-known 'Wet' factory alongside [1930-32]) of the Boots chemical plant."[34] **(Figure 13)** Williams's building designs were far more advanced and innovative in their use of concrete than those of contemporary architects in Britain, although he understandably did not share The New Brutalists concern with architectural history and his work was hardly admired by architects at the time. Yet L-148 provokes both trivial and powerful affiliations to Williams's work and to The New Brutalism that go beyond Banham's and are too striking to ignore. For example, the curved, perforated concrete canopies at the Boots "Wet" factory, take advantage of molding techniques much like those used for the louvers at L-148. But perhaps the closest relative to both The New Brutalism and L-148 is Williams's Peckham (Pioneer) Health Center. Despite its conventional exterior, that building demonstrates one variation of Banham's attitudes toward the spatially defining role of structure, similar especially to Hunstanton. Unlike the Boots Factories (which the Smithsons' denied knowledge of until Banham mentioned it) the Peckham Health Center (which the Smithsons certainly knew) shares a scale and perhaps a structural and even a social and political ethic with the Hunstanton School.[35] **(Figure 14)** The rigorous application of concrete structure as the primary organizational device of the Health Center is conceptually analogous to the Smithsons' use of steel frames (and their application of "plastic theory" in collaboration with Ronald Jenkins of Ove Arup) at Hunstanton. More significant is how Williams's seemingly "formal" plan actually is entirely unconventional in its disposition of program and its subdivision of space in the service of a progressive social program. L-148 deploys basic structure similarly to adapt Chinese factory models and working conditions. Finally, Williams's design, however architecturally naïve, of a wavy front façade is a crude anticipation of the imaging of The New Brutalism, a strategy that is much more elaborately and elegantly developed at L-148 in ways that extend and advance the understanding of architecture as topological image-making.

Its image is certainly the most striking aspect of L-148, as demonstrated by the architects' numerous photographs of cyclists and pedestrians distracted by the building as they pass. L-148's primary elevation can be conceived as another emergence of The New Brutalist effort to redefine architecture's complex relationship to vision in terms of imaging. The concern with image, and L-148's specific variation on the theme in contemporary Chinese culture, invites us to reconsider the ways that The New Brutalism became wrapped up in the early- to mid-1950s with the aesthetic experiments of the Independent Group, and by implication the emergence of Pop. Banham offers two versions of that relationship. The 1955 version draws on ideas and attitudes developed among the Independent Group to open up powerfully speculative potential for an architecture of mass appeal, while his 1966 revision of his concept of *une architecture autre* overly constrains the definition of Pop, and distances it from the specifically architectural devices and criteria that motivate his earlier discussion of

13, 14_ "Proto-Brutal": While Banham suggests that Sir Owen Williams's Boots Dry Factory (1935-8) was the only "conceivable precedent" for the Smithsons' Sheffield project, Williams's Pioneer Health Center (1933-5) may be the more likely relative to both the New Brutalism and L-148.

topology and image. Banham's presumption in 1966 that a turn toward Pop was in effect a turn away from the original version of The New Brutalism was an unfortunate erasure of his earlier insights, and L-148 is vivid evidence of his mistake. Banham's shift in devotion to a new contemporary 1960s Pop led him to propose the diametrical contrast between the two *This is Tomorrow* projects. In his desire to be current, he both falsely settled and further confused the issue by overly simplifying the relationship between The New Brutalism and the Independent Group. In 1956, in his review of *This is Tomorrow,* Banham was closer to the truth.

In the fifty years since his book was published, numerous examples – in architecture, art, and art history – help us see Banham's blindness. A parallel, or some might say aberrant, version of the pop image, but one which is much more visible and pertinent today, appears in the varied work of Gerhard Richter, which emerged out of his own twisted relationship to Pop, which first coalesced in the 1963 exhibition, *Living with Pop: A Demonstration for Capitalist Realism.* An intriguing characterization of Richter's work would align it with the New Brutalists' preoccupation with the ongoing emergence and historical evolution of the replicable image in mass media. Examples range from Richter's blurred photo paintings, to his scrape paintings, to his more recent strip paintings, and even his glass sculptures. **(Figures 15-16 , page 85)** Richter's image is not a representation but a kind of echo or repetition of immanent organization. Troels Wörsel has explained Richter's early work, which involved painting new images of photographs, as "pictures of pictures, pictures of pictures associated with text, pictures of press photos, amateur photos, aerial photos – all of this material that advertises its 'imageness.' In other words, they are paintings that, as pictures, represent pictures."[36] That simultaneous evasion and iteration of representation brings painting closer to architecture's allusive manner of dealing with visual analogy and affiliation. Intriguingly, Richter once explained his own attitude toward painting in quasi-architectural terms: "The act of making should occur without inner involvement, like crushing stones or painting a building. Making is not an aesthetic act."[37] Looking back from the 1980s, with eyes and attitudes shaped by several decades of changes in image culture, the Smithsons similarly described what they, Paolozzi and Henderson were after in their approach to Parallel of Life and Art: "planes of images were suspended from the ceiling or angled against the walls, as if floating in space ... Images happening beyond images: the introduction of a plane, the tempo of whose images were contrapuntal to that of its setting."[38]

This all informs my understanding of the concrete logic and image of L-148 as is both iterative (the arrays, patterns, and grids that distribute and connect its discrete components) and cohesive (the diagrams, uses, and assembly processes of its structure and spaces). This understanding can be augmented by Roland Barthes's concept of "the neutral" which he describes as a strategy of "outplaying the paradigm" or "everything that baffles the paradigm."[39] By paradigm, Barthes means a fundamental structural opposition, which normally operates by actualizing one term over the other to produce meaning. The neutral evades prioritizing either term. One of his myriad examples of outplaying a paradigm is the Taoist explanation of human minds as mirrors, but not in the sense of a mechanical and passive device that replicates and responds in kind. Instead, it imparts an "action without appropriation" by "replying without retaining."[40] This kind of neutral mirroring intensifies image. In this kind of mind repetition produces an *imago* which refuses the concepts of character or identity and their implication of uniqueness or individuality. Similarly, Richter's images are all unique, but also all seemingly after the same image, and thus after each other. Richter's images baffle and twist meaning. Are they like twisted baffles? They are released from the oppositional binary logic of the negative, or copying. Richter's images echo, or repeat without retaining, their source image and its specific claims.[41] He insists on this by using a variety of devices of reflection or doubling as a schema. Some are internal to the format of the painting; some occur as part of its production or process; some operate in relationship to a source image. It is a strategy that simultaneously clarifies and distributes the image. Perhaps Barthes, as usual, says it best: "one doesn't protest against an image, that is useless. What can be done is to drift by displacing the paradigm."[42] Like the Smithsons and Richter, the neutral is wryly contrarian and anti-dogmatic, taking an interest in key issues and preoccupations of the moment, but with a twist, with a difference. "Everything about the neutral is about sidestepping assertion,"[43] Barthes writes, but not by neutering, or being non-descript: rather, the neutral is capable of "intense, strong, unprecedented states."[44] In other words, by being brutal. Such is the logic and effect of L-148.

15, 16_ "Neutral Images": Repetition and replication produce images which refuse the concepts of character or identity, and simultaneously clarify and distribute with no implication of uniqueness or individuality.

Endnotes

1 Banham, "The New Brutalism," *Architectural* Review (December 1955): 361.
2 Banham, "The New Brutalism," 361.
3 Banham, "The New Brutalism," 358.
4 Banham, "The New Brutalism," 357.
5 Banham, "The New Brutalism," 358.
6 Banham, *The New Brutalism: Ethic or Aesthetic?*, London: The Architectural Press, 1966, 134.
7 Banham, "The New Brutalism," 357.
8 Banham, "The New Brutalism," 356.
9 Banham, "The New Brutalism," 357.
10 Banham, "The New Brutalism," 361.
11 Banham, "The New Brutalism," 361.
12 Banham, *The New Brutalism: Ethic or Aesthetic?*, 68.
13 Banham, *The New Brutalism: Ethic or Aesthetic?*, 69.
14 Banham, *The New Brutalism: Ethic or Aesthetic?*, 68.
15 Banham, "The New Brutalism," 361.
16 Banham, "The New Brutalism," 361.
17 Banham, "The New Brutalism," 361.
18 Banham, *The New Brutalism: Ethic or Aesthetic?*, 68.
19 Banham, "This is Tomorrow," *Architectural Review* (September 1956): 186.
20 Banham, "This is Tomorrow," *Architectural Review* (September 1956): 187.
21 *This is Tomorrow*, London: Whitechapel Gallery, 1956, n.p.
22 Banham, "This is Tomorrow," *Architectural Review* (September 1956): 187-8.
23 Banham, "This is Tomorrow," *Architectural Review* (September 1956): 188.
24 Banham, "This is Tomorrow," *Architectural Review* (September 1956): 188.
25 Banham, *The New Brutalism: Ethic or Aesthetic?*, 64.
26 Banham, *The New Brutalism: Ethic or Aesthetic?*, 65.
27 Banham, *The New Brutalism: Ethic or Aesthetic?*, 65-6.
28 Banham, *The New Brutalism: Ethic or Aesthetic?*, 64.
29 See "'Patio and Pavilion' Reconstructed," *AA Files* 47 (Summer 2002): 37-44.
30 Also, significantly, the Smithsons made similar associations among their projects and in relationship to Mies in *The Shift: Architectural Monographs* 7, (London: Academy Editions): 1982. The book assembles buildings and projects from 1950 to 1967, and includes previously unpublished images as well as retrospective commentary (a contemporary history of a sort) on their motivations and preoccupations at various times in their career.
31 See Banham's books, *Guide to Modern Architecture* (London: Architectural Press, 1962) and *Age of the Masters*. (New York: Harper and Rowe Publishers, 1962).
32 Reyner Banham, *Theory and Design in the First Machine Age* (Cambridge: MIT Press, 1980), 321.
33 Banham, "The New Brutalism," 358.
34 Banham, *The New Brutalism: Ethic or Aesthetic?*, 43.
35 For a detailed discussion of the social politics of modern architecture in Britain between the wars, see Elizabeth Darling, *Re-Forming Britain: Narratives of Modernity before Reconstruction* (Oxford: Routledge, 2007).
36 Troels Wörsel, "Image, Window, Mirror," in *Gerhard Richter: Image after* Image, eds. M. Holm, A Kold, M. Marcus, P. Tøjner, Humlebaek, Denmark, Louisiana Museum of Art, 2005, 79.
37 The remark, made in 1971, is quoted in Coosje van Bruggen, "Gerhard Richter: Painting as a Moral Act," *Artforum* 9 (May 1985): 86.
38 Smithson, *The Shift*, 10, 12.
39 Roland Barthes, *The Neutral: Lecture Course at the College de France (1977-1978)*, trans. Rosalind Krauss and Denis Hollier, New York: Columbia University Press, 2005 [2002], 6.
40 Barthes, 182.
41 Alex Bacon offers a compelling version of the visual neutrality of Richter's work. "Reflections on Gerhard Richter: Painting 2012." www.brooklynrail.org/2012/11/art/reflections-on-gerhard-richter-painting-2012. Add date accessed. "Like the child that crawls into a discarded cardboard box to take imaginative respite in its neutrality from the intense pressures to conform to one cultural demand or another, the best abstract work makes no impositions on, or demands of, the viewer, but instead allows him or her to reflect back on the nature of these demands, and on his or her place within them. ... In this way certain abstract work like Richter's is not merely compensatory, because it does not in fact offer to replenish something proposed to be lacking—phenomenological plenitude, for example—but rather suggests to hold, as best it can, all of these terms momentarily in abeyance—that is its radical neutrality."
42 Barthes, 73.
43 Barthes, 44.
44 Barthes, 7.

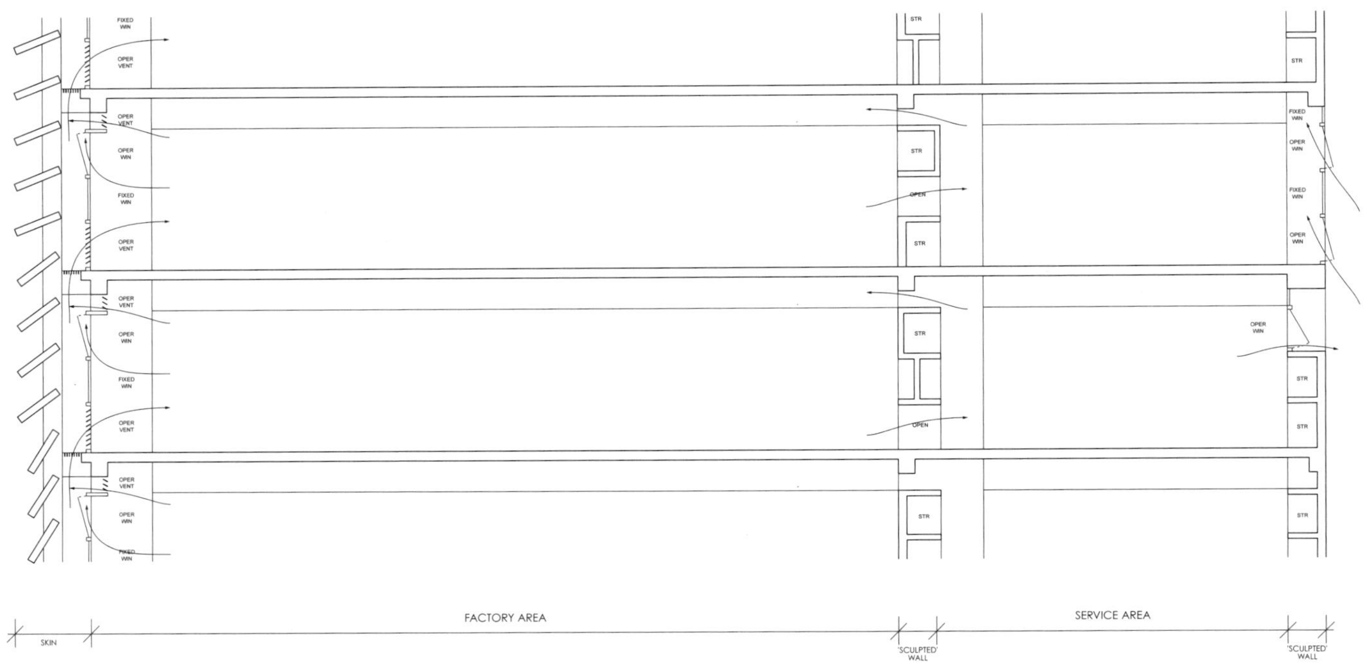

1_ Partial building section describing air movement

Glazing

Mehrdad Hadighi

We worked with a local glass manufacturer to design and specify all glazing for the building. Our aim was to reduce the number of shapes that required unique frames and glass sizes. The extreme of this solution would have been to use a single repetitive window type. This would have obviously been the most cost-effective solution. However, we were interested in the tension between the repetitive mass-produced element and a playful, nuanced result, much like a manually-crafted object. In addition, we were interested in naturally ventilating the building in order to overcome the unbearable heat that would result from regular power outages, knocking out all air conditioning systems during the summer. We worked with a number of operable window types to bring in air in each floor low to the floor and ventilate it through higher openings. **(Figure 1, opposite page)** This system included two operable window types and one fixed type. By increasing this number to nine, we were able to glaze the entire building for light and ventilation, and yet keep a playful, almost-random appearance.

This is most visible on the north façade of the building. Using the nine glazing types and a system of varying depths, we created twenty-seven different window types, creating a façade totally governed by the repetitive structure of the building, yet playful in its configuration. **(Figures 2-3, page 90)** Vertically organized stacks of stairs, bathrooms, elevators, and lobbies, while all being lit and ventilated by the glazing system, create a compositional play that does not rely on the repetitive nature of their structure. The three varying depths of the glazing system allowed us to create varying intensities of light and shade. Some windows are glazed flush with the concrete creating a smooth outer surface; others are mounted in reverse, pushing the glazing into the façade. Others are truly recessed by virtue of their location in one of the carvings. The result is a façade that while respecting and abiding by the repetitive structure of the building, and while using a limited set of glazing parts, results in a composition of variable surface depths, with plays of light and shadow. **(Figures 4-5, page 91 and figures 6-9, pages 92-93)**

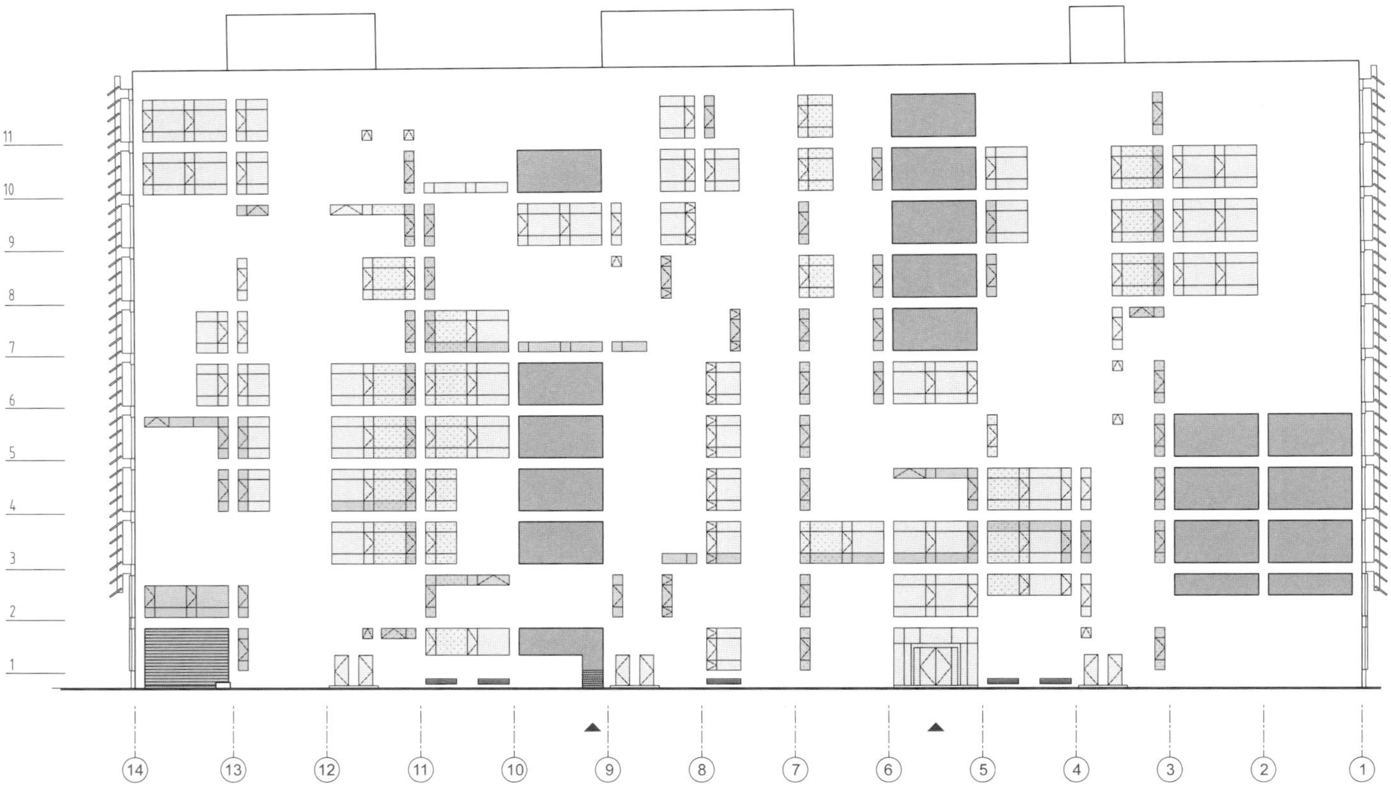

2_ North elevation

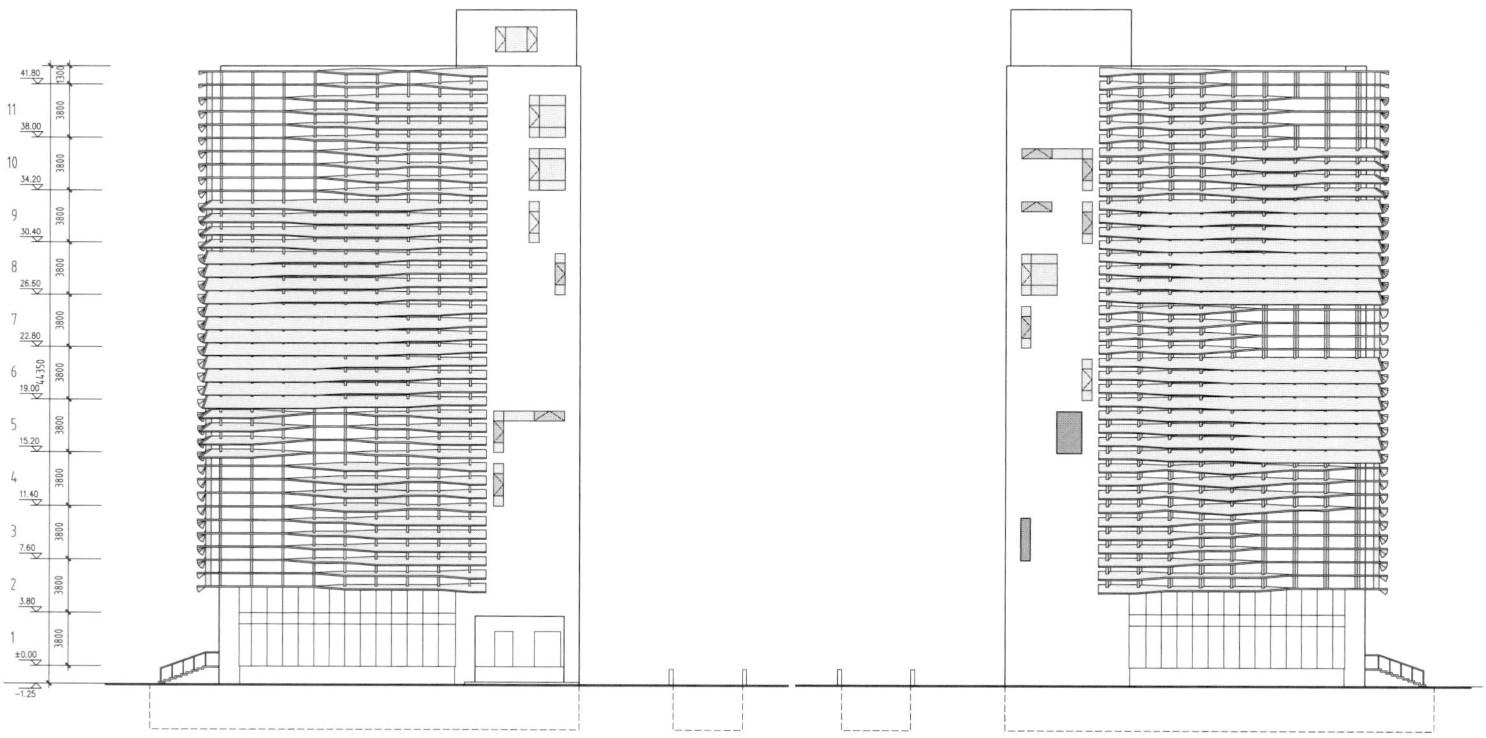

Translucent glazing
Flush glazing
Recessed glazing
Opening

3_ East and west elevations

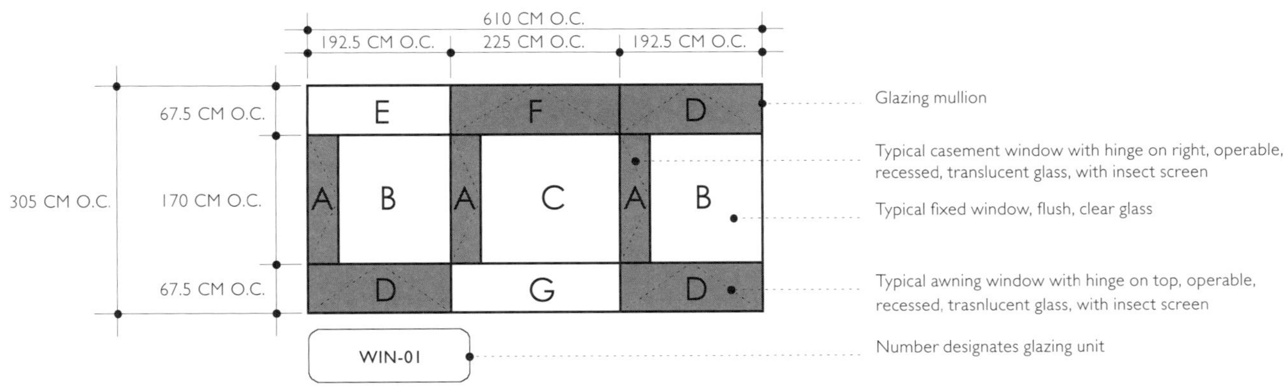

4_ Detail elevation - Glazing unit

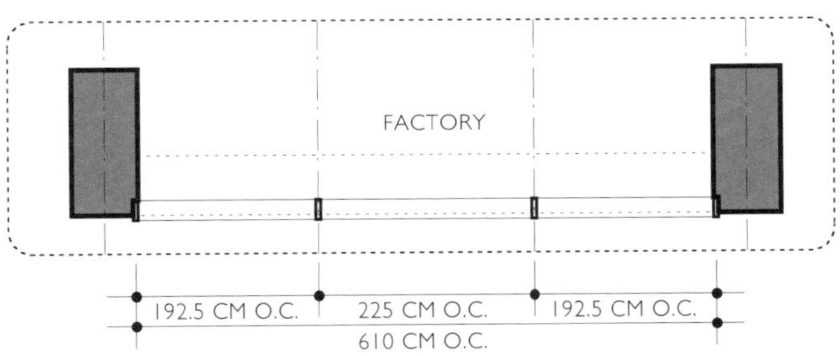

5_ Key plan - South elevation glazing unit

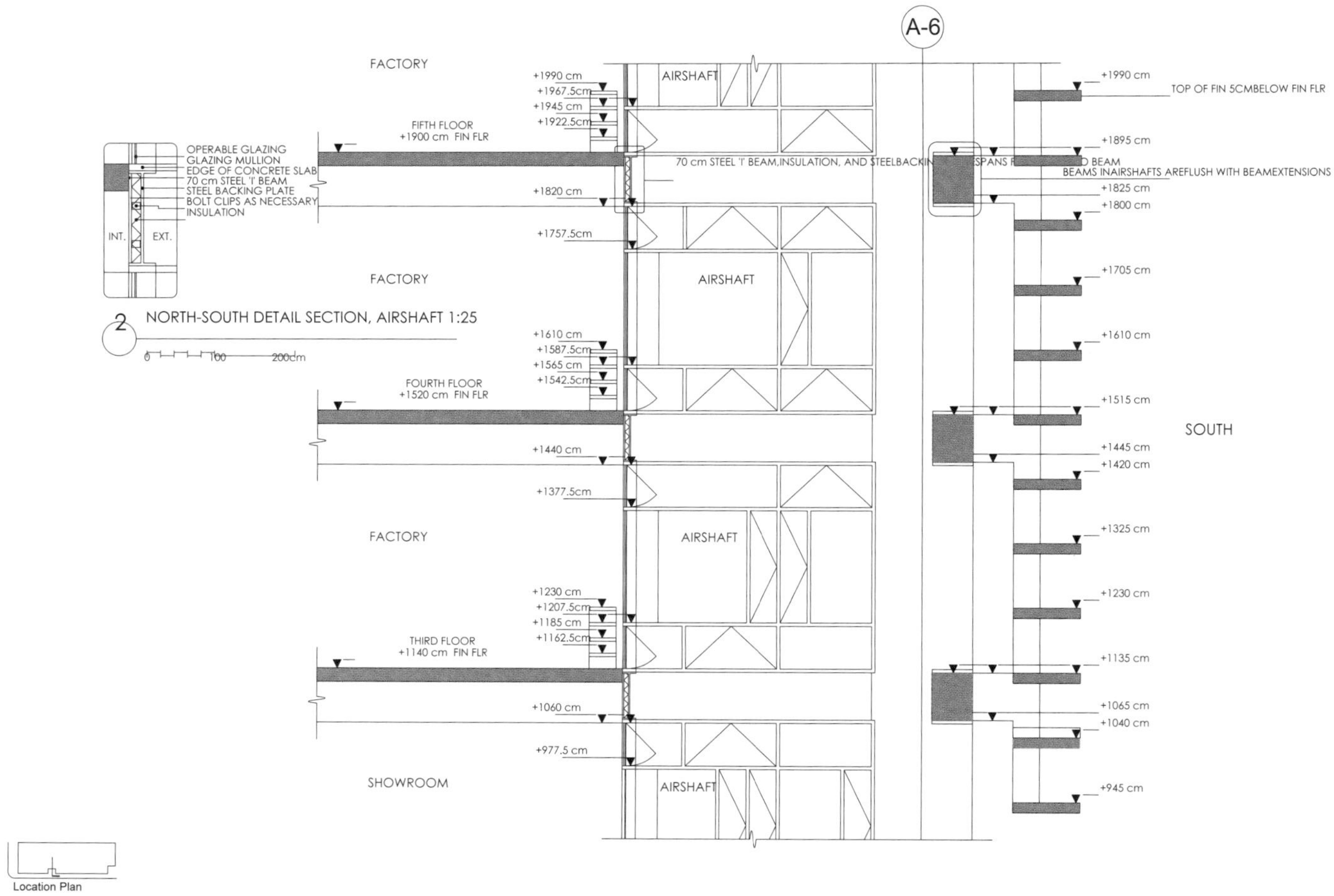

6_ North-south detail section, airshaft 1:50

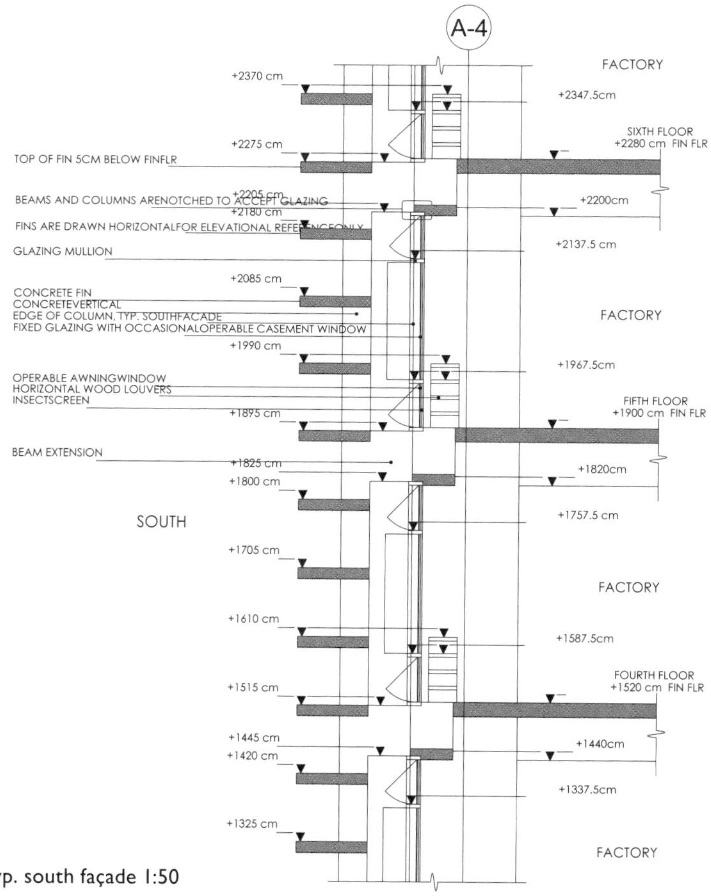

7_ Detail section A-4, typ. south façade 1:50

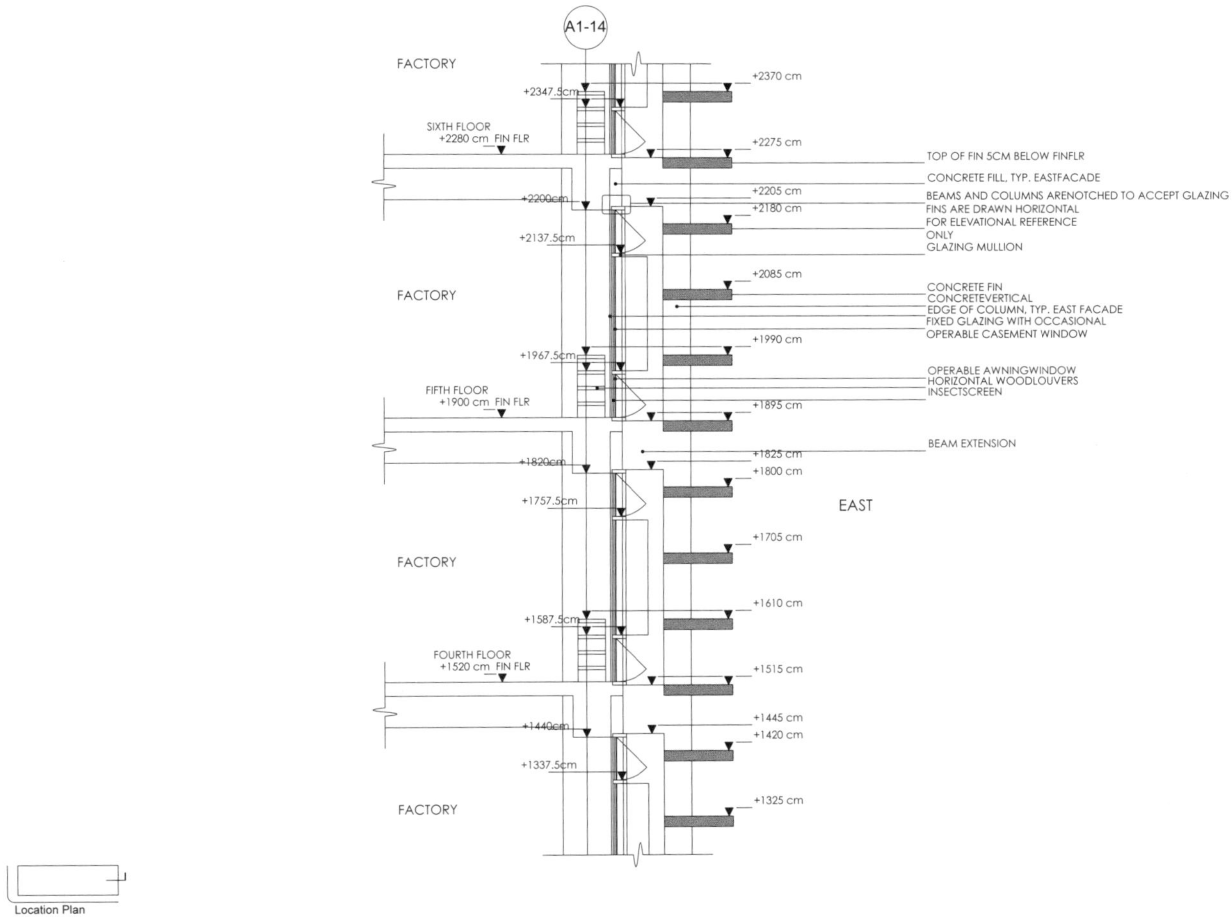

8_ Detail section A1-14, typ. east façade

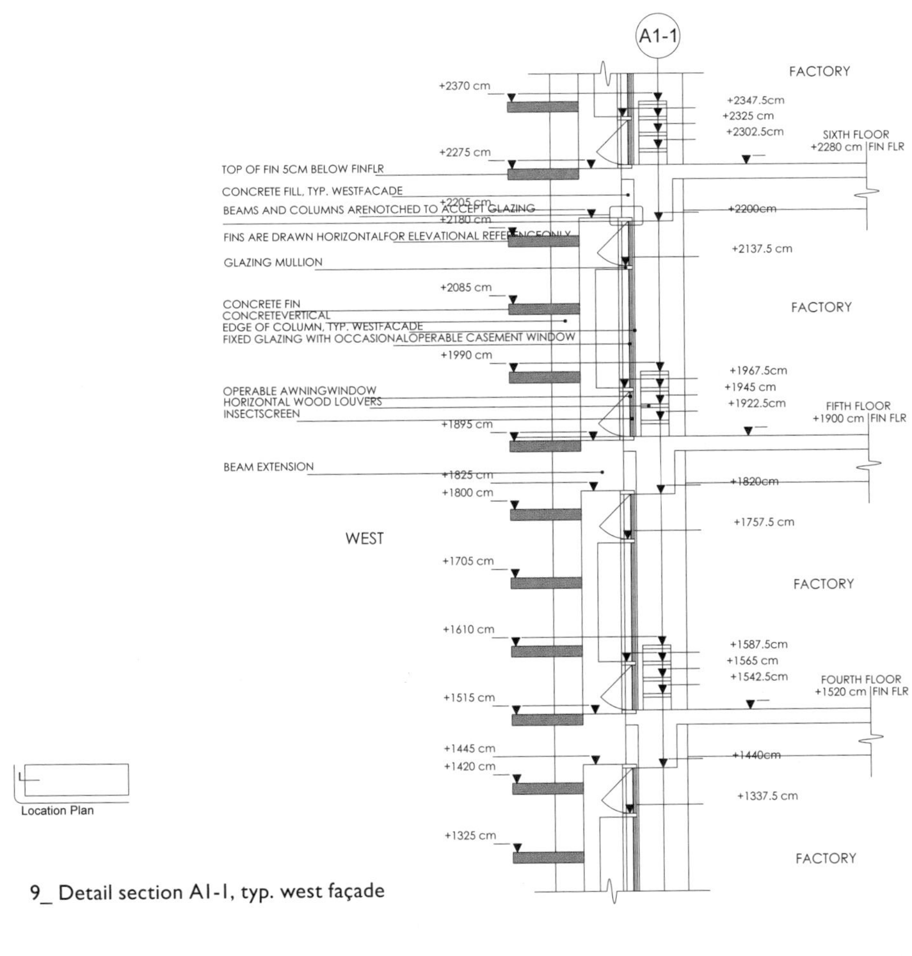

9_ Detail section A1-1, typ. west façade

Interlude
Marc J Neveu

Architecture / Clothing

The analogy between clothing and architecture, especially at the beginning of the twentieth century, is well documented.[1] There are similarities that are hard to ignore. A building, not unlike clothing, encloses our lives and protects us from the environment. Both help to mold, communicate, or even mask, our identities. To fashion, the verb, as in to make something, certainly relates to the modulation of space. Clothing has structure but can also be deconstructed. Construction drawings are akin to patterns – abstract two dimensional drawings used to convey the operation of fabrication. Contemporary fashion houses operate similarly to architecture offices with the names of designers standing in for the corps of workers producing the products – one wears a dress by Prada, just as they go to the museum designed by Koolhaas. Similar technological advancements changed the production of both. The introduction of mass produced cotton in the 1830's and the development of reinforced concrete in the mid-nineteenth century forever altered the material landscape in both disciplines. So too did the invention and wide-scale use of the sewing machine (patented in 1851) and the introduction of the safety elevator by Elisha Otis in 1852. One could argue that architects produce haute couture – made to order, high quality, singular, and often expensive designs.

Clothing unlike architecture, however, is mass produced. It is relatively less expensive. It can be made by hand. Fashion has seasons. Each season a new line is produced. Clothing changes much more frequently than a building lasts. To buy, wear and then discard a t-shirt is simply not the same as the erection and razing of a building. Buildings are situated in a time and a place. Clothing is much more temporal. One can change one's clothing to match the weather. One cannot change architecture as easily or in the same way. Is there something more to the analogy between architecture and clothing that is productive? The following essay will briefly discuss the analogy, and more specifically that between the façade of a building and clothing. The essay is divided into three parts. The first looks at the historical use of the analogy to determine "appropriateness." The second explores the role of dressing and masking in the work of Semper and Schinkel. The third offers a case study that proposes a more productive relationship between the architecture and clothing.

Appropriateness

First, a story.

An eighteenth-century Venetian milliner had ordered the latest and most fashionable hat from Paris for a wealthy client. When the hat arrived, his wife fell in love with it and begged her husband to make a copy of it to send to the client, who, at this point, was on holiday in the country, so that she could wear it. After a bit of discussion, he agreed, sending his client the replica and giving his wife the original to wear. That night, while wearing the hat, she was very well received all over Venice and her hat was praised. The next morning, after hearing what an amazing reception his wife had received at the *casini* the previous night, the hat-maker decided to wear his wife's hat to the Rialto while he made his morning errands. Strangers snickered as he walked by; others could barely stop themselves from bursting with laughter while they spoke with him. Confused, he asked a friend why everyone was mocking him. His friend suggested that he might want to go home and give his wife her hat back. Still a bit confused, the hat-maker asked, "But why, my wife received so many compliments last night?" The friend responded, "Sure, the hat is wonderful and lovely, on your wife. But, on you, a serious man doing business at the Rialto, it is ridiculous!"

This story was told to architecture students in Venice, sometime around 1750 by Carlo Lodoli.[2] It was in the context of understanding the appropriateness of the function and representation of a building façade. Lodoli believed that the nature of materials should be clearly expressed and was, therefore, critical of the use of the orders as the vocabulary of a building. He believed the original tectonic system of the orders was wood, implying an appropriate way of making relative to material. Lodoli critiqued the classical orders as a misrepresentation of the material nature of a stone construction. The stone order inappropriately mimicked wooden construction. To build a façade in stone that references a system of wood construction is as ridiculous, according to Lodoli, as that serious young man doing business on the Rialto wearing his wife's hat.

The relationship between clothing and architecture and the resultant "appropriate" expression goes as far back as Vitruvius who described columns that were adorned in matronly robes to express a feminine appearance, which was appropriate to the building.[3] Appropriateness, however, is always an issue of custom and situation. It is easy to see differences in clothing over time as well in various contexts. Wearing a burka or baseball hat is not, inherently, appropriate but may be considered so, or not, in various contexts or situations. Around the same time Lodoli was telling tales, Adam Ramsay questioned the possibility of a universal standard of appropriateness in his dialogue "On Taste."

An artist may, by Palladian receipt alone, without any taste, form a very elegant Corinthian pillar, as a cook, without any palate, and by the help of the housewife's vade mecum only make an unexceptional dish of beef a la daube. These rules are plainly no more then analysis of certain things which custom has rendered agreeable; but do not point out to us any natural standard of beauty or flavour, by which such things, whether pillars or dishes, could have been originally contrived to answer the purpose of pleasing. I should be exceedingly glad to hear a reason why a Corinthian capital clapt upon its shaft upside-down should not become, by custom, as pleasing a spectacle as in the manner it commonly stands.[4]

Claude Perrault's description of arbitrary beauty reaches a similar conclusion. Perrault defined arbitrary beauty as "determined by our wish to give a definite proportion, shape or form to things that might well have a different form without being mis-shapen and that appear agreeable, not by reasons within everyone's grasp, but merely by custom and the association the mind makes between two things of a different nature."[5] The Orders, for Perrault, were considered a part of this (arbitrary) type of beauty. Hundreds of years later, Le Corbusier, in his seminal work – *Vers Une Architecture* – claimed that the architectural "styles of Louis XIV, XV, XVI or Gothic, are to architecture what a feather is on a woman's head; it is sometimes pretty, though not always, and never anything more."[6] In *L'art décoratif d'aujourd'hui,* published two years later, Le Corbusier continually uses the variability of clothing styles to demonstrate the validity of the contemporary over all that has come before. He offers a comparison between the dress of Louis XIV and the President of the Republic to demonstrate issues similar to Lodoli's apologue of the hat.

There is, however, a twist.

For Le Corbusier, "Construction has undergone innovations so great that the old 'styles' which still obsess us, can no longer clothe it [architecture]; the materials employed evade the attentions of the decorative artist."[7] The critique is more specifically focused on the possibility of new materials and methods of construction, and not simply an appropriate expression or style. Le Corbusier, building on nineteenth century precedents, calls for few forms of architecture that relate to new forms of construction. This, of course, is not new. Otto Wagner, an architect who was also interested in the discourse around clothing, argued that, "new methods of construction must also give birth to new forms."[8] In many ways, these calls echo developments in building technologies. The roles traditionally performed by the exterior wall – structure, ventilation, and light – are all replaced by the beginning of the twentieth century. The advent of steel structural systems allows for the exterior wall to clad, rather than support, the interior; advances in electronics and lighting bring continuous and even artificial light to interiors; and the development of mechanical heating and cooling (most often through the movement of air) eliminated the need for windows to be operable. In short, the tectonic clarity and purpose of a wall is put into question when it no longer needs to perform in ways it had historically.

The question is less of style, per se, than the relationship between the representation and production of a building. This was Lodoli's critique of Greek architecture and it is an argument that continues through the nineteenth and twentieth centuries. In other words, the performance of a façade, and indeed the criteria by which we assign meaning to a building, has changed over time. The representational capacity of building is replaced by various means of production. With this, amongst other issues, there is an emergence of the truth-claim to making architecture that is questionable at best. How can material systems that are inherently artificial be used "truthfully"? Though many architects value and even subscribe to this truth-claim, most buildings, however, rather than actually revealing the true nature of construction often present a tautology of construction. Brick no longer supports an arch, but is hung like a shroud covering a structural skeleton or concrete frame.[9] Lacking any performative need beyond keeping the interior and exterior environments separate, a series of questions regarding surface and meaning arise. How then does one find meaning in an architecture that is simply shrouded in material? What makes one enclosure more appropriate than the next?

Masking Purpose

Perhaps the most often referred to claim to the relationship between clothing and architecture was made by Gottfried Semper who argued for a correlation more primitive than Laugier's Hut. Semper, in fact, rejected Laugier's primitive hut in lieu of a more complex archetype comprised of four motifs: hearth, mounding, roofing and enclosure.[10] Each is a component of the "Carib" hut from Trinidad that was displayed at the Great Exhibition in 1851 and each related to a particular technical craft. The hearth houses fire and is the element around which familial and religious groups gather. It is related to ceramics. Mounding raises up the hearth from the ground and is related to masonry. Roofing shields the flame from the elements above. The system of roofing gives rise, according to Semper, to carpentry. Finally, enclosure, protects the flame and is related directly to textiles. The enclosure was composed of non-load bearing filler: textiles, weaves, hides or wattle. Semper explained that *wand* (wall, partition, screen) relates etymologically to *gewand* (dress, garment, clothing). He, however, prioritizes *bekleidung* (dressing or cladding), which relates to *kleidung,* (clothing) in his investigations.

The first (and longest) section of his massive *Der Stil in den technischen und tektonischen Künsten oder Praktische Ästhetik* (1860-63) is on textiles and there Semper makes the comparison clear. Helmets and crowns are paired with acroteria; vestments with taeniae; woven objects with mosaics, etc. Semper relates human clothing to architectural clothing through the crucial notion of dressing. To be clear, this is not about fashion. Semper used the term fashion pejoratively – linking it to rapid circulation of style. Rather the principle of dressing was, for Semper, representative of the structural and symbolic essence of a building. It was not possible to conceive of decoration and "art of form" as distinct. Only with "complete technical perfection, by judicious and proper treatment of the material according to its properties," could the artistic creation transcend material for its larger social and cultural purpose." The transition is historical; branches are plaited, fabric is woven, textiles are hung to divide space, and polychrome woven walls became painted surface. Here, and in opposition to Lodoli's position, the Greek's use of wall dressings became "spiritualized." The orders are not inappropriate; they are of a higher order. Beyond simply dressing, the surfaces were in fact masked. This masking coincides, for Semper, with the development of Greek drama. Semper explains: I think that the *dressing* and the *mask* are as old as human civilization and the joy in both is identical to the joy in those things that drove men to be sculptors, painters, architects, poets, musicians, dramatists – in short, artists. Every artistic creation, every artistic pleasure presupposes a carnival spirit, or to express myself in a modern way, the haze of carnival candles is the true atmosphere of art.[11]

Prior to Semper, and arguably different in nature, the writings and building of Karl Friedrich Schinkel offer an interesting lens by which to view Semper's idea of dressing as it relates to masking. Similar to others mentioned above, Schinkel thought that, "Every principle age has left behind its architectural style." And then asked the obvious follow up question, "Why should we not also seek to discover a style from our own age?" His initial approach, however, was to define a morphological taxonomy of constructional forms related to the epoch in which they arose. He argued that "construction forms the starting point of design" and thus "everything essential must remain visible," because "it is through the characteristic of visible constructional parts the building receives something living." This was not, however, an argument for the truth-claim to materials, nor is this simply construction. Building must be enhanced. He continued, "Very different from sensible pleasures, forms thereby awaken moral-spiritual pleasures, which arise partly from the pleasure of ideas evoked, partly from the delight that unmistakably arises through the mere activity of clear understanding."

Schinkel described this sort of approach with the word *zweckmassigkeit* (purposive-ness). From Kant's *Critique of Judgment* purposive-ness is "the causality of a concept with respect to its object."[12] Schelling and Schlegel also develop the term and refer back to Cicero. It is functional, but, again, there is a twist. The example used is that of gabled roof. Originally, the gabled roof was put in place to shed rain. Over time, according to Cicero, the form of the roof becomes associated with a higher, and perhaps more poetic, meaning of the Temple. So much so, that, according to Cicero, if a Temple were built in heaven (where no rain falls) there would still be a pediment. It is this same thinking that informs the architectural expression at the Altes Museum in Berlin designed by Schinkel. The eighteen massive columns that front the building do more than simply support the roof of the arcade. The scale of the columns, and front porch in general, situate the building on the Lustgarten in relation to the Royal Palace and Berlin Cathedral. Two enormous frescoes sit within the porch set the iconographic narrative for the building, which continues internally through to the central pantheon. A section of the building shows the intention is not to express the clarity of construction or materials, but to elevate both.

A more contemporary example of Schinkel's *zweckmassigkeit* can be found in the work of Mies van der Rohe. It is not difficult to relate the intention of the over scaled beams that span Crown Hall to be similar to the colossal columns that front the Altes Museum. A more obvious example might be the bronze I-beams attached to the façade of the Seagram Building. The metal supports imply a structure that is buried within the wall beyond. They have no purpose beyond signifying (or masking?) the purpose of the structure within. Mies referred to this as "skin and bones." He did not articulate clothing per se, but his position seems to have foundations in the nineteenth century conversation around dressing and masking.

The Fabric Tower by Atelier Manferdini (Guiyang China, 2008) offers a more contemporary perspective and one that is clear about its use of clothing as an analogy. According to Manferdini's website the 150,000 sq.ft. housing tower is, "an articulate response to the site's natural landscape and its minority cultures, expressing a contemporary, progressive, creative, and original vision of local traditions."[13] The local tradition to which Manferdini is referring is the elaborate silver head dresses worn by the women of the minority Miao population. One can easily understand Manferdini's interest. The headdresses are elaborately woven silver and offer a veritable history of the wearer. Families begin saving for the headdresses when the girls are young. The actual fabrication of the headdresses may take months and in the end may end up weighing ten to twelve pounds. Though I would not argue the elegance of Manferdini's solution – how does one argue elegance? – Manferdini's translation from the headdresses to the housing tower is a somewhat loose translation. There is an obvious scale difference between a headdress and a tower; the original import of the headdress (as a historical record) is lost; radically different materials require different approaches to fabrication, structure, and production. The symbolic import (free of scale and/or material considerations) trumps all others. This position, intentional or not, also seems to be rooted in nineteenth century discourse. Each of the examples above, however, requires some knowledge of cultural context that is referenced. How might the analogy between clothing and architecture be productive but not simply referential?

Performance

Lafayette 148's headquarters in Shantou, I would argue, actually does what Manferdini claims to do, but in a much more appropriate manner. Hadighi and Ng's building in Shantou also seems to be wrapped in woven fabric, and, is indeed enclosed by a double façade. The façade also claims a relationship back to a native culture, though not of ritual headgear, but from the local tradition of concrete construction. In Shantou, the architects found themselves in a situation in which concrete construction was the norm (though often concealed) and on-site poured in place concrete production was not prohibitively expensive and actually more efficient. This is evidenced in the façade construction. Rather than mass-produced singular pieces, as in the Fabric Tower, the architects along with local contractors, designed re-usable formwork from which family of concrete fins were produced. The fins were hung at various angles, flowing into one another, to produce an array of effects. The effects are, however, not simply visual. The façade operates as a shading device and masks operable windows. The combination of shading and airflow though the building has resulted in a cost savings of 40% in energy consumption relative to similar manufacturing buildings in the region. Air conditioning is used infrequently and only to reduce humidity. The play of the façade also relates to the performance of the program within, revealing just enough to keep you wanting more.

Each of the fins were produced on site and with local labor. Holes were punched out of the concrete fins. The holes themselves are a representation in braille of the company's name. Although this might be a rather oblique reading, the holes in the fins perform in a number of fascinating ways. The holes lighten the twisted fins to be more easily hung. During the construction process, chain pulleys looped through the holes and allowed for the fins to be picked up, transported and finally set in place. The holes also provide for a play of shadow on the interior surfaces. Contrary to the unfortunately all too typical scenario that finds large western companies exploiting the inexpensive, and often unethical, labor practices in China, at Lafayette 148 the architects are dependent upon but also develop the local tradition. The product is not, however, exported for profit but rather stays on site. In fact, this mode of fabrication could only occur in a situation such as that exists in Shantou.

At Lafayette 148, the façade is less formal than performative. The building does not rely upon the mask of cultural reference for significance. The design of the façade, rather, considers natural and artificial light conditions, airflow, the nature of materials, the process of construction, the carbon footprint of material use, the relationship to program, and even the branding of the company. The façade is not masking performance or relying upon cultural reference but is appropriately tempered to consider the building's situation, culturally and physically, as well as the occupant's experience. It is these ways that the analogy between clothing and architecture may be appropriate but not necessarily fashionable.

Epilogue

Although architects have been drawing analogies between architecture and clothing for centuries, at Lafayette 148, the analogy is reversed. In an unusual but wonderful twist, the building's façade has informed the branding of a recent clothing line for the company.

1 See especially Mark Wigley, *White Walls, Designer Dresses: The Fashioning of Modern Architecture* (Cambridge, MA, MIT Press), 1995, and *Architecture in Fashion,* Eds. Deborah Fausch, Paulette Singley, Rodolphe El-Khoury, and Zvi Efrat (New York, Princeton Architectural Press), 1994.

2 The original apologue was oral. Only after Lodoli's death were the apologues published by Andrea Memmo in *Apologhi, immaginati e sol estemporaneamente... Lodoliana.* (Bassano: Remondi), 1787. For a complete translation into English see Marc J Neveu "Architectural Lessons of Carlo Lodoli" unpublished dissertation, McGill University, 1995.

3 See Vitruvius Book IV ch. I The "unadorned" is considered masculine.

4 A. Ramsay, "On taste," *The Investigator* (London: 1762; reprint, New Haven: Yale University Press, 1972), 33.

5 Claude Perrault, *Ordonnance for the five kinds of Columns after the method of the Ancients.* Translated by Indra Kagis McKewan (Los Angeles, Getty Center for the History of Art and the Humanities, 1993): 51.

6 Le Corbusier, *Towards a new Architecture,* Tr. by Frederick Etchells (New York, Dover Publications: 1986): 37.

7 Le Corbusier, *Towards a new Architecture,* Tr. by Frederick Etchells (New York, Dover Publications: 1986): 286.

8 Otto Wagner, *Modern Architecture.* Translated by Harry Francis Mallgrave (Los Angeles, Getty Center for the History of Art and the Humanities, 1988): 93.

9 The Exeter Library is an interesting example here. Even though Kahn asked the brick what it wanted to be (an arch), the building has sandstone lintels above each of the openings on the interior. There are, however, arches on the exterior.

10 Gottfried Semper, *The Four Elements of Architecture.* 102-103.

11 Gottfried Semper, *Style in the Technical and Tectonic Arts,* TR. Harry Francis Mallgrave and Michael Robinson, (Los Angeles, Getty Center for the History of Art and the Humanities, 2004): 438-39.

12 Immanuel Kant, Kant's Critique of Judgement, Tr. J.H. Bernard (2nd ed. revised) (London: Macmillan, 1914): (§10, 220).

13 "Atelier Manferdini - Fabric Tower." http://www.ateliermanferdini.com/work/#/still-1-4-4-1-1/ accessed 01July 2016.

Modulating

Mehrdad Hadighi

The building is located in a sub-tropical climate in Shantou, a city on the Eastern coast of Guangdong province of China on the banks of East China Seas. **(Figure 1)** Being on the sea, the air quality and movement are generally good. The city enjoys average temperatures between 57-82 degrees Fahrenheit, with hot and humid summers with extreme temperatures in July and August between 95-104 degrees Fahrenheit. Humidity in the region ranges between 75-85 percent, making summer months very hot and humid. Shantou, a city of over five million, with a history of textile manufacturing, due to the growth in manufacturing sector, suffers from weekly power outages. Given the climate and the regularity of the power outages, we knew that we had to design a building that was able to naturally control its interior temperature, ventilation and lighting. **(Figure 2)**

Shantou is in the northern hemisphere, close to the equator. The building's southern façade is in the sun in the winter months, and during the summer its southern, eastern, and western façades are in direct sunlight, with east and west receiving both high and low angle sun in the summer. In order to shade the interior of the building from the hot summer sun, we introduced a series of fins horizontally spanning the east, south and west sides of the building from the ground floor to the roof. The primary role of the fins is to keep the hot summer sun out of the building. The architectural vocabulary of the fins was derived from the textile studies conducted earlier in the project. **(Figure 3, page 106)** With slight modulation of the relationship of the warp and weft, we were able to maintain the horizontal continuity of the fins, and at the same time, manage the low sun angles on the East and West façades with deeper vertical members. **(Figures 5-6, pages 106-107)**

As the project progressed, we recognized that we could utilize the fins for multiple means, creating air currents on the façade, cooling the airspace behind the fins, and also modulating the level of interior lighting. We wanted to keep the fins as open as possible at the location of the carvings, allowing as much light into the depths of the building. We also knew that certain

1_ World map, locating Shantou in relation to the equator
2_ General view of the city of Shantou

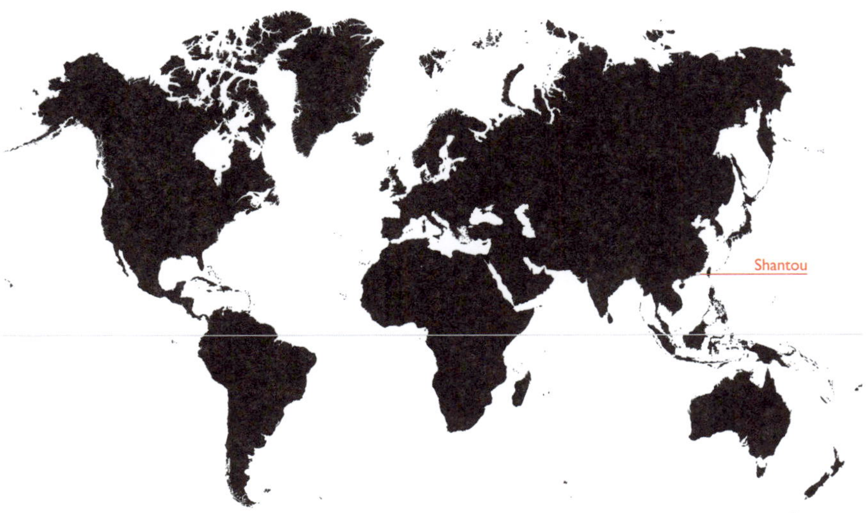

3_ Textile studies

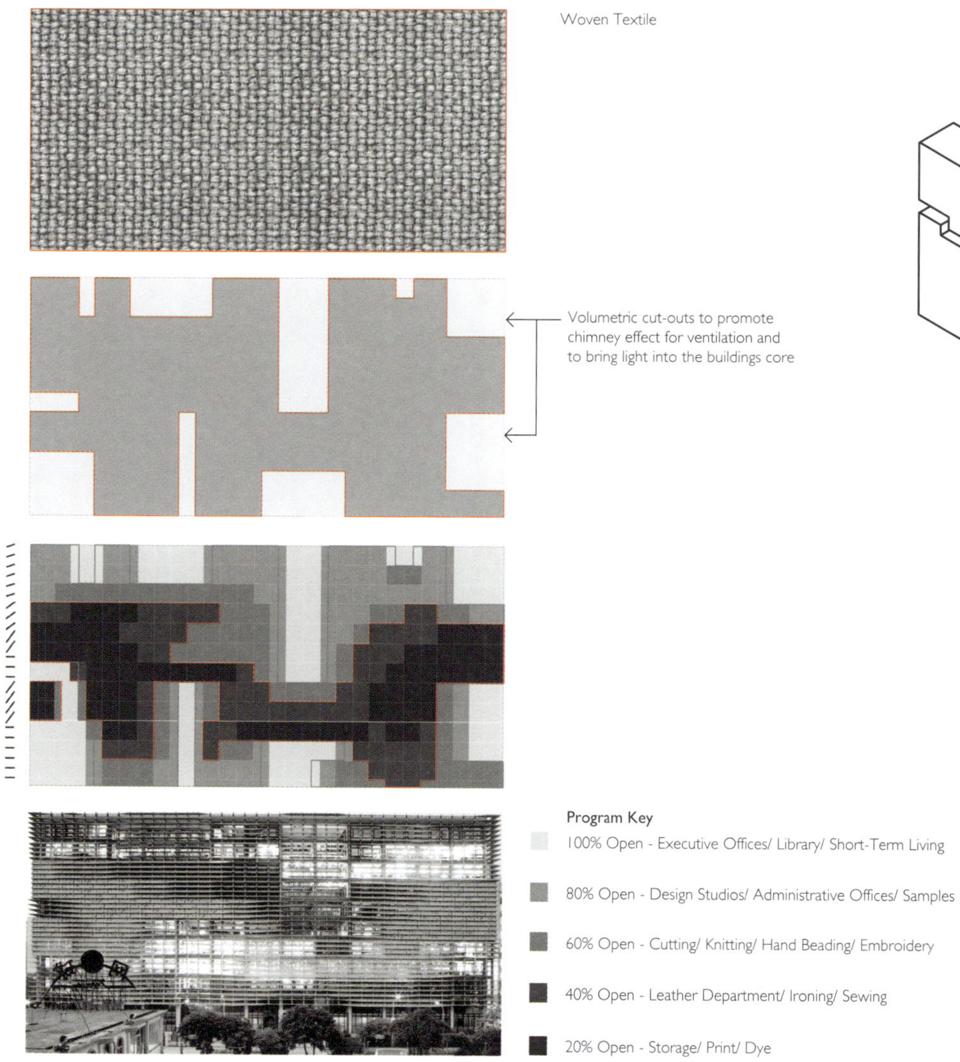

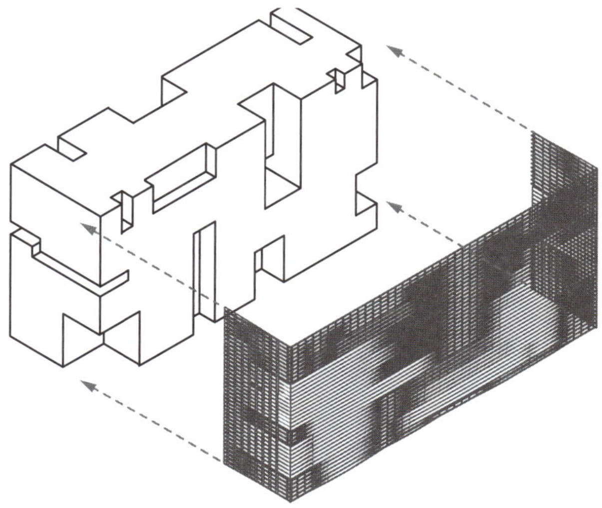

4_ Program façade study. Left

5, 6_ Sectional diagrams of South, East and West fins. Above and right

programs of the factory required very controlled levels of interior lighting. Through a careful study of the programmatic layout of the building, which in itself is a diagram of the operation of the factory, we were able to devise a system of angles for the fins that permitted the modulation of the interior light levels. Given the different level of lighting required for different factory practices – sewing, bead-work, dying of fabrics, and leather curing – we, once again, devised a limited set of possibilities for the angles of the fins. In combination, however, the angles created the appearance of a continuous variable sinuous twist with no repetitive element visible.
(Figure 4, opposite page and Figures 7-8, page 108)

Concerned with the weight of the fins, we decided to perforate them, wherever possible. We also recognized that as a result of perforations and the top layer of the fins being exposed to the sun, we would get a natural movement of air upward, sucking hot air from the airspace between the fins and south of the building glazing. The Venturi-effect created by the large volume of air between fins moving upwards through the small perforations creates a constant flow of warm, heated air, upward. This desirable environmental effect convinced us further about the use of the perforations. As we tried to figure out how to construct the constantly varying, sinuous twists, we realized that the perforations also assisted in relieving material surface tension as the form-work material accommodated the three dimensional curvature of the fins. We then knew that the perforations had to also serve a branding aim for the building in order to ensure that they would happen, despite the additional cost and labor involved in their making.

We designed a Braille text that spelled the name of the fashion label, Lafayette 148, repeated across the fins. The rhythm of the repetition of the Braille text, however, is mis-aligned with

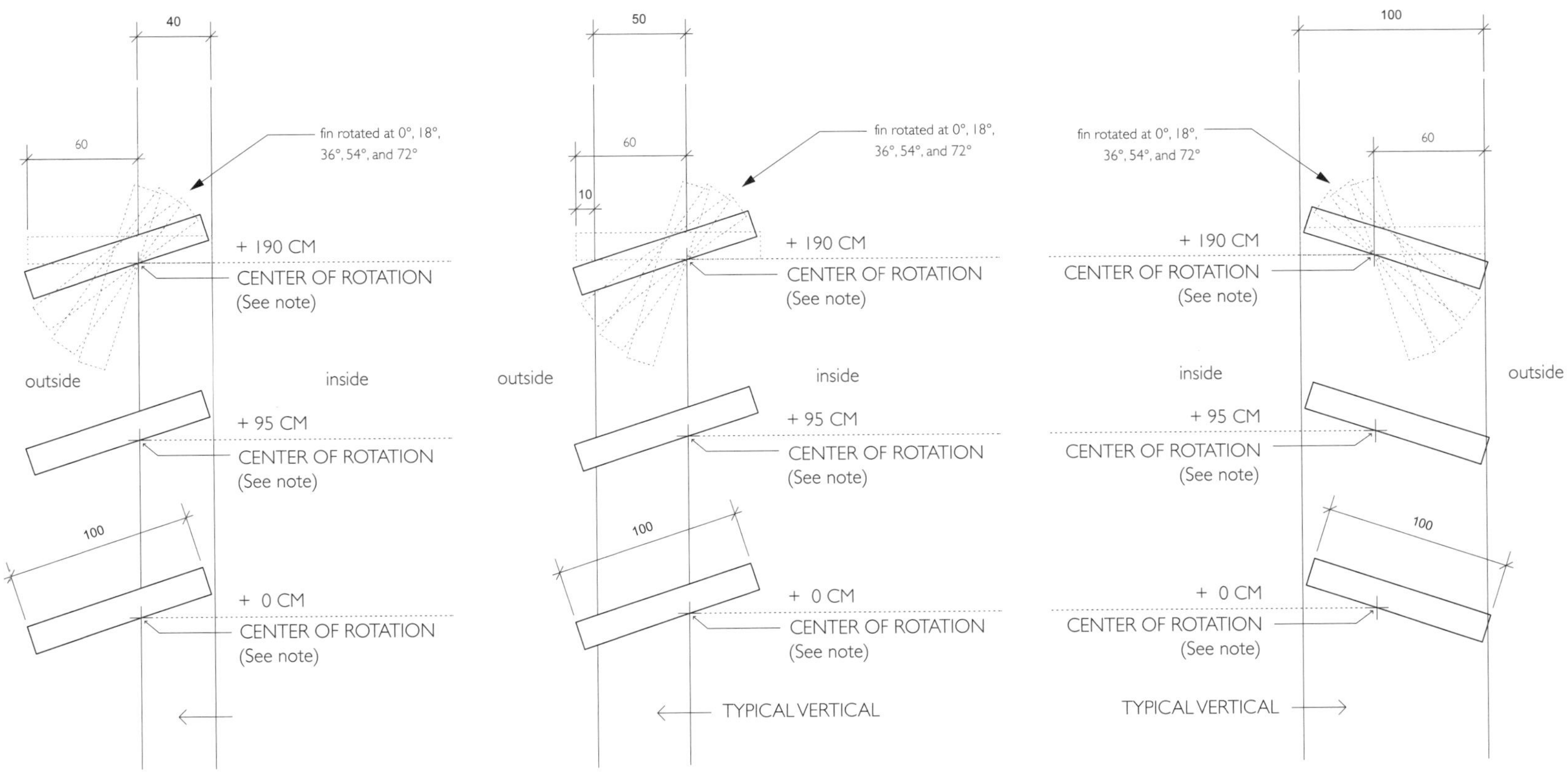

Detail Section
Center of rotation for West façade
Scale 1:25

Detail Section
Center of rotation for West façade
Scale 1:25

Detail Section
Center of rotation for East façade
Scale 1:25

Note:
This series of fins have been rotated to 18 degrees increments between each verticals. The center of rotation is located at the BOTTOM of the fin for WEST, SOUTH, and EAST facade. The center of rotation must be 60cm from the outer most edge of the fin (FROM THE OUTSIDE) in order for the fins to align properly all around when rotated. This is also necessary for the Southeast and Southwest corners to intersect properly.

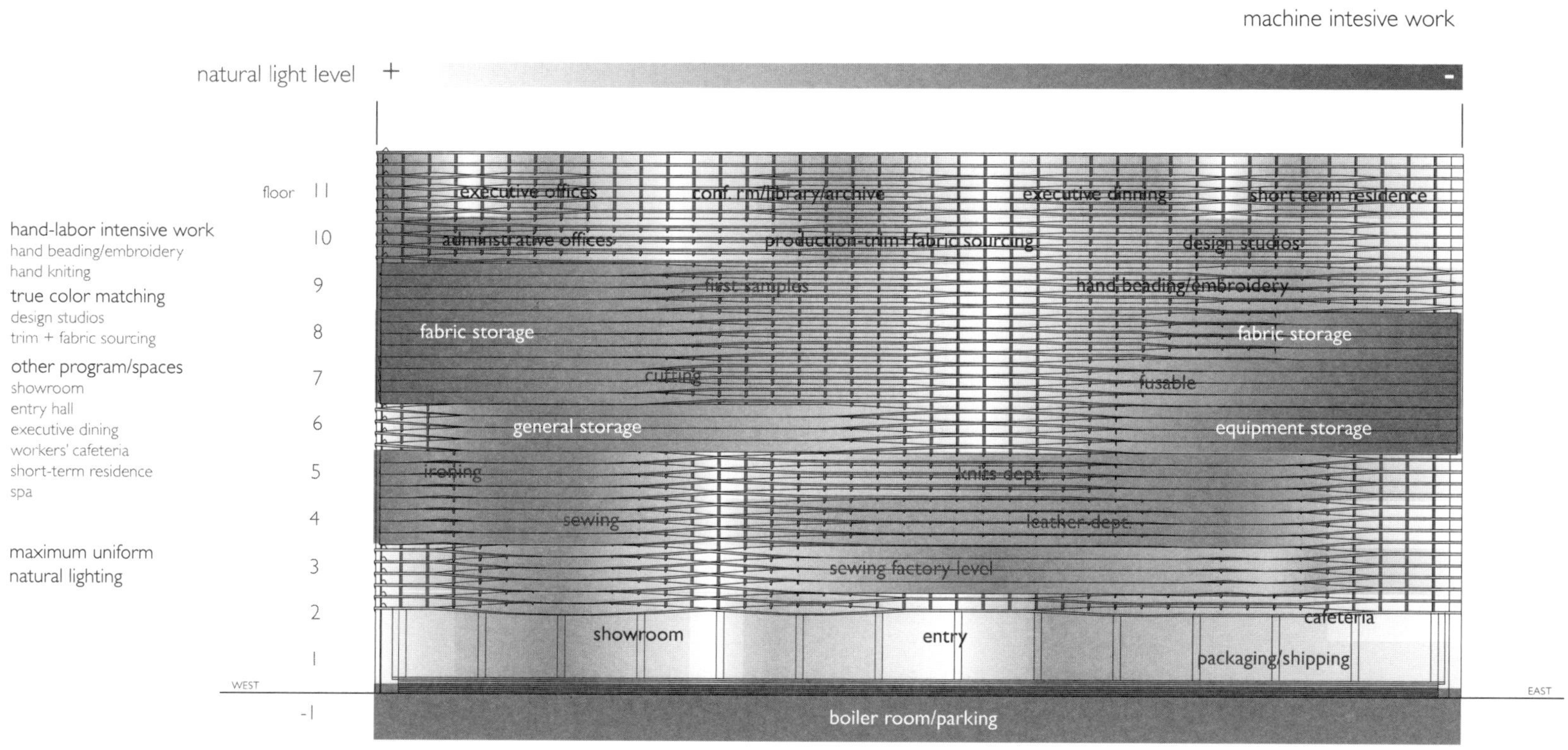

7_ South façade with programmatic diagram for various lighting conditions

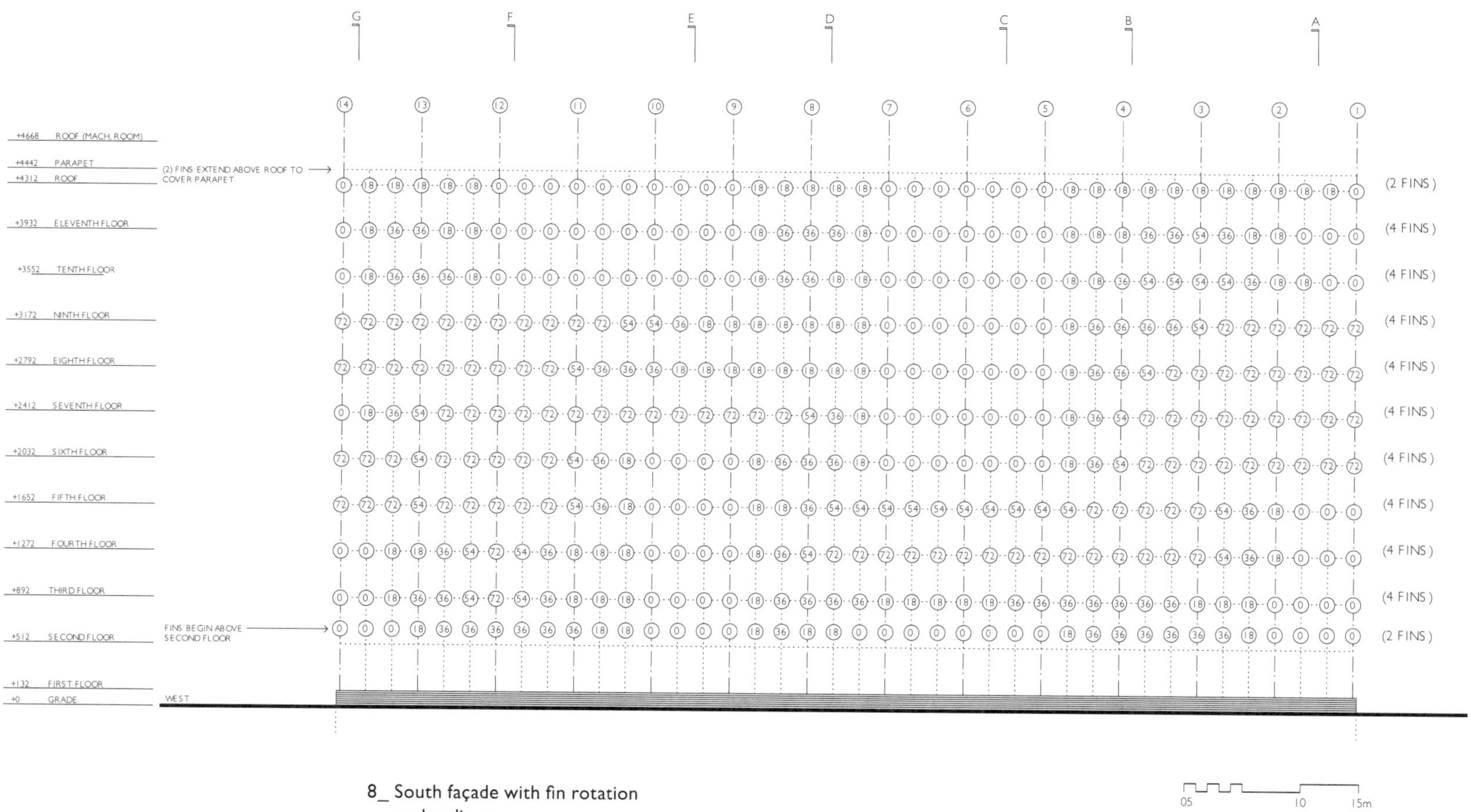

8_ South façade with fin rotation angles diagram

the rhythm of both the fins and the structure of the building, creating the appearance of a randomized composition. **(Figure 9 and Figure 10, page 110)**

We tested full-scale alternatives for the construction of the fins in our office in Buffalo, NY. The technical challenge was to form the four-hundred foot sun-shading fins that ran horizontally on the south, east, and west façades of the building, and do so in a continuous manner. Adding complexity to this effort was our decision to make the fins in reinforced concrete, manually cast, with perforations and twists against the horizontal axis. Our thoughts, initially, were to cast each fin in-situ, and continuously for its entire length, which seemed to be an almost Herculean effort. To that end, we explored fabricating the formwork across two fin segments, trying to fix as many points as possible within an orthographic environment so that the movement of the front lip of the fin could be correctly described and constructed. We tested multiple thicknesses of plywood in order to see which thickness lent itself best to the particular twists that we were proposing. We constructed the edges of the formwork from laminations of multiple layers of plywood that could slide against each other, so that all different curvatures of the front lip may be produced from the same formwork. We also constructed the vertical members, knowing that the horizontal datum had to be marked and followed on the vertical members as the orthographic source of all curves. We recognized that each vertical member at the point of connection to the fins had to provide a transition space between the different curvatures of the fins. This characteristic alone turned out to be the most difficult to achieve. In effect, each vertical member created enough of a "flat" spot for each curve to end and transition to the next curve.

Our plywood thickness tests ensured that the proper amount of transition was provided with the given thickness to create a seamless continuous curve across the entire face of each fin, from east to south to west. We produced a system of formwork that would be re-usable

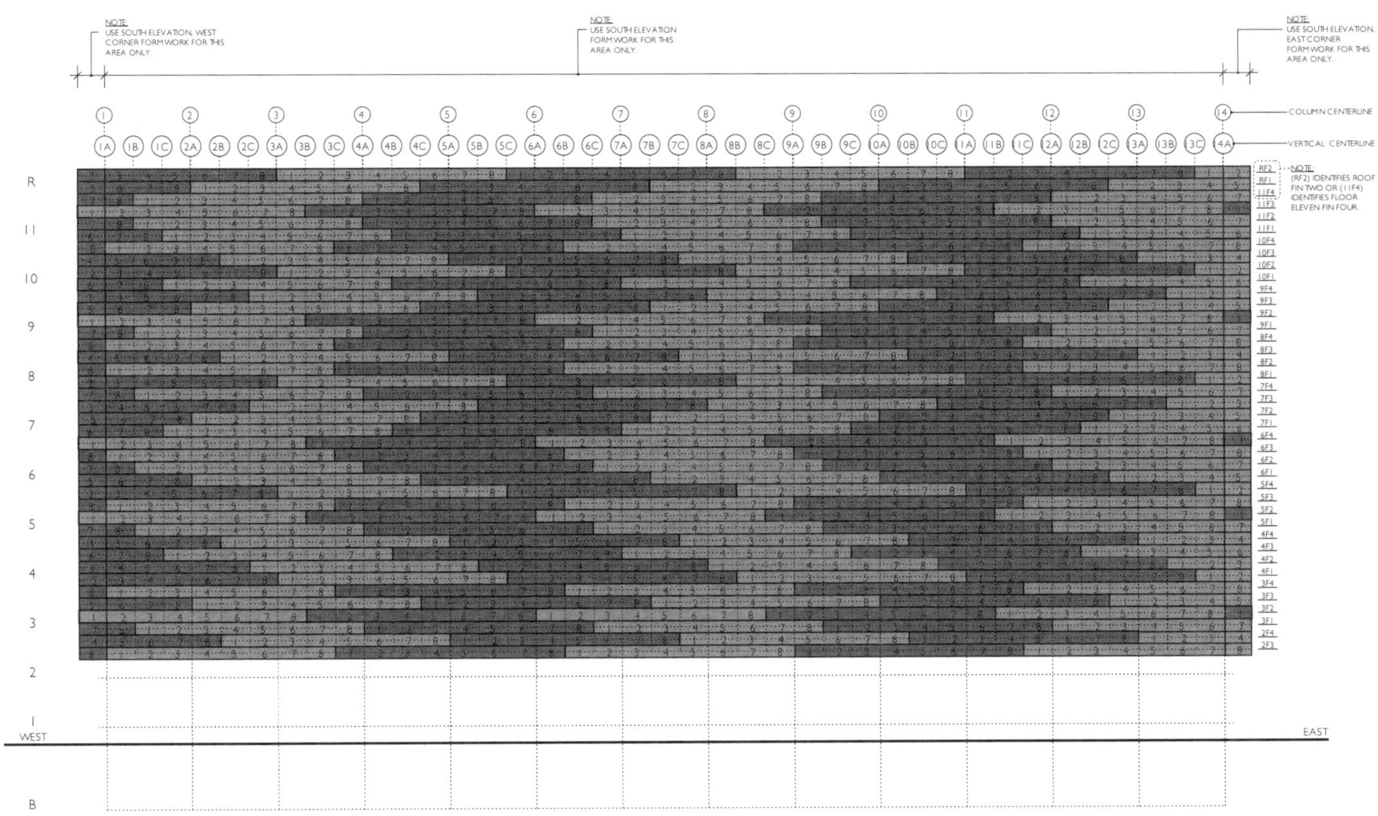

9_ South façade with braille diagram

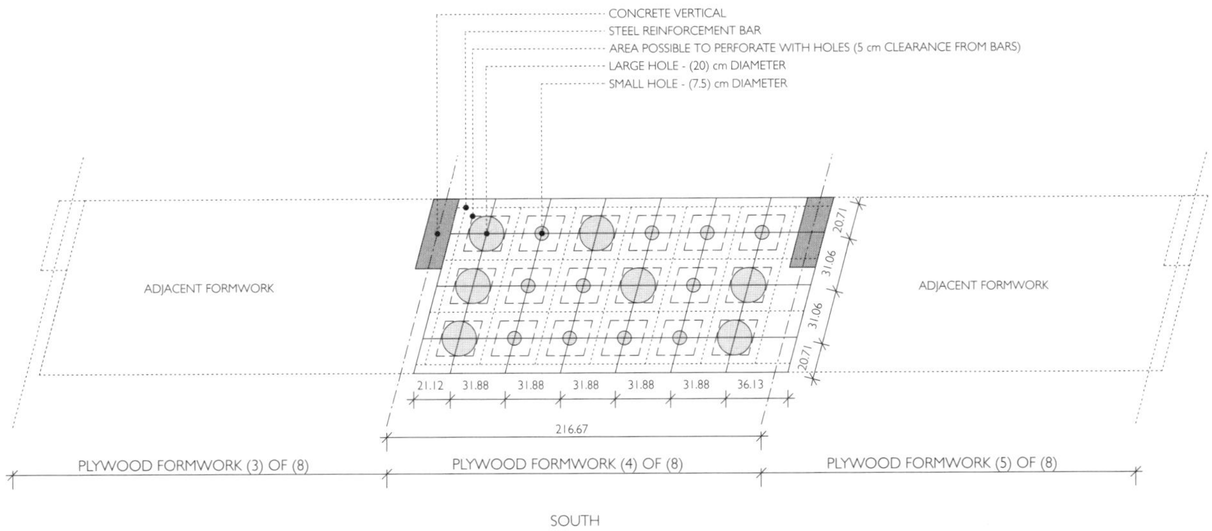

Detail plan - Hole patter for fins

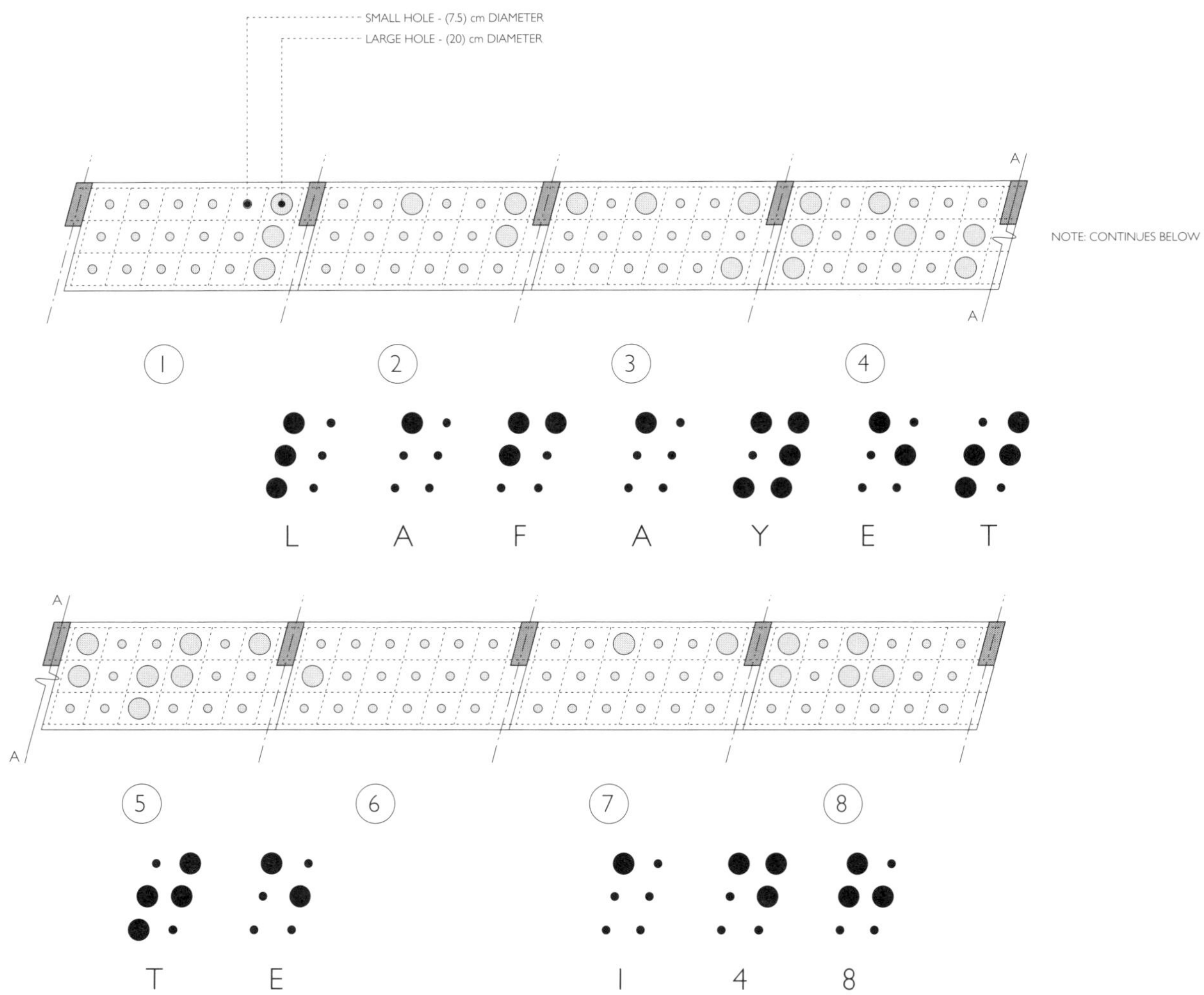

10_ Braille diagrams

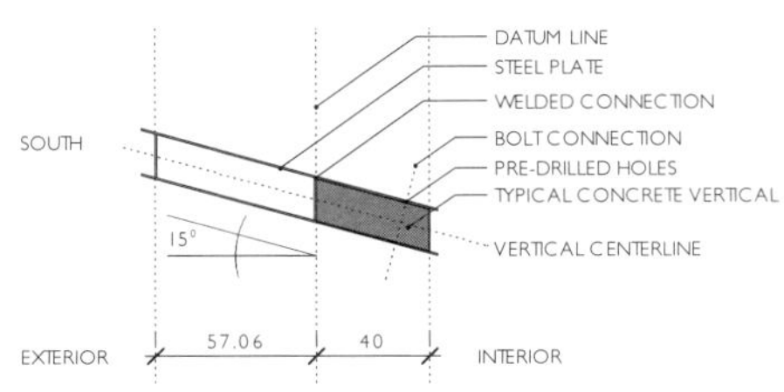

Plan: 18 Degree clip fabrication

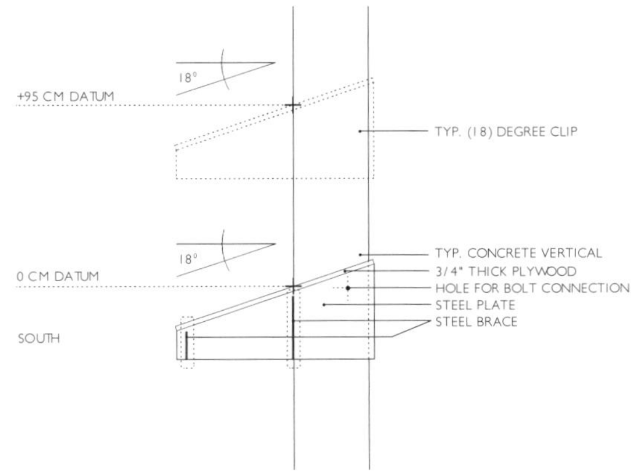

Detail plan - Hole patter for fins

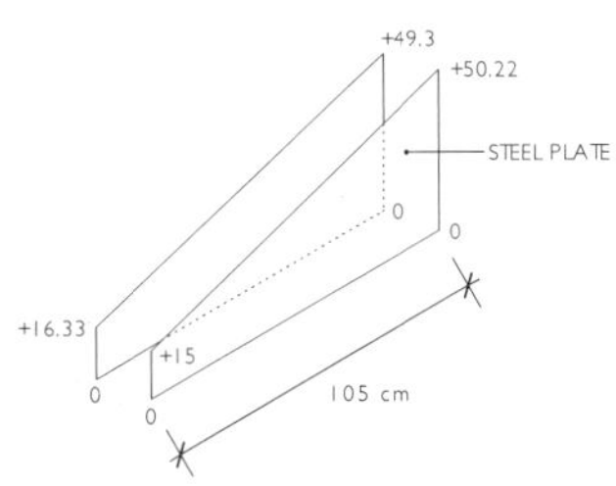

Step 01 - Cut plates

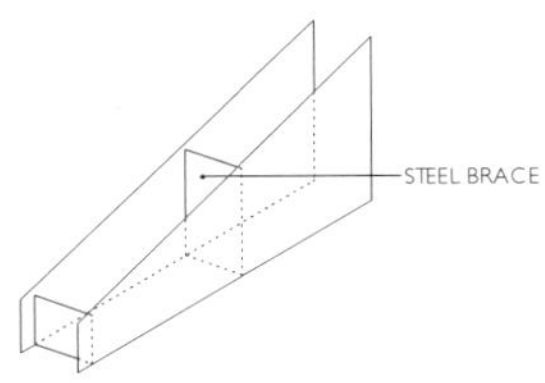

Step 02 - Add brace

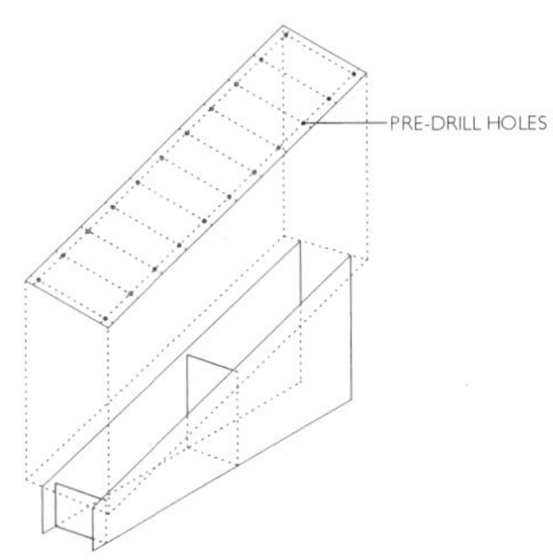

Step 03 - Drill holes

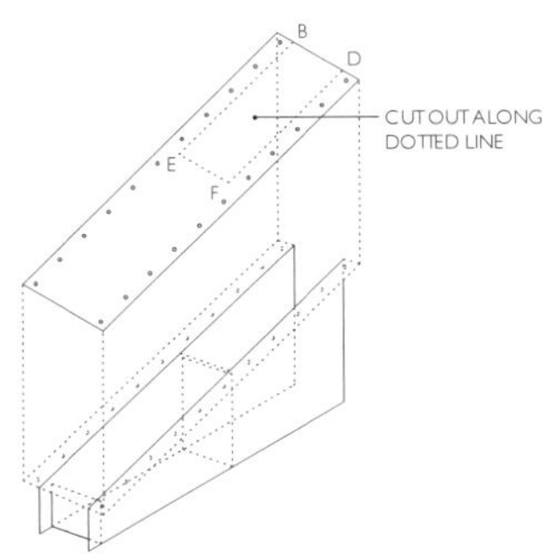

Step 04 - Cutout notch

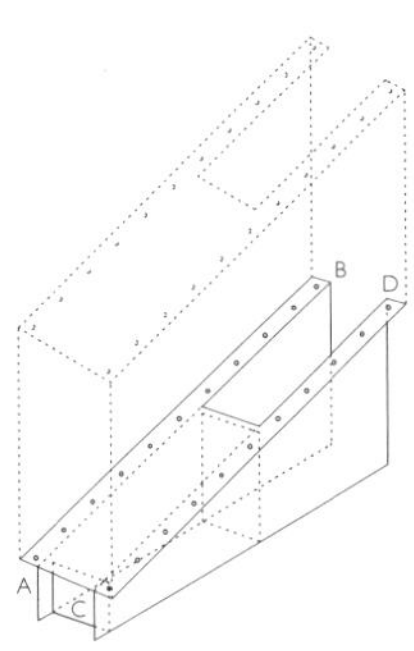

Step 05 - Torque plate

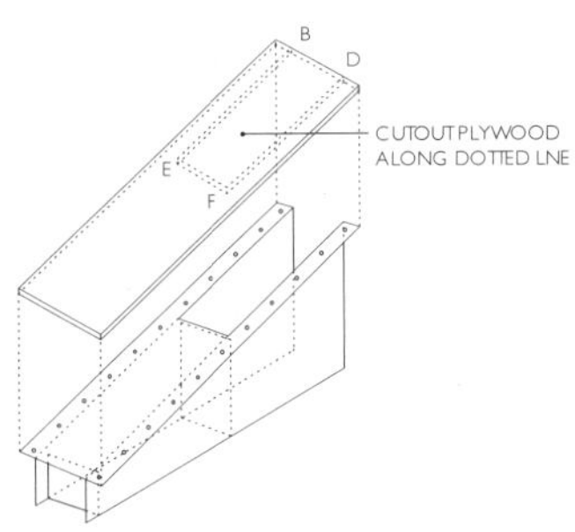

Step 06 - Cutout notch

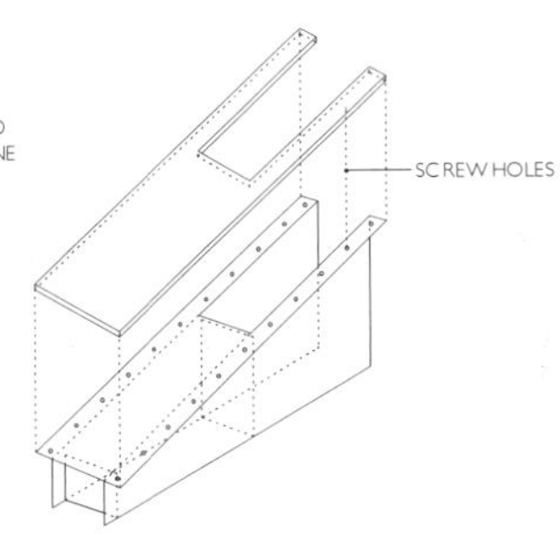

Step 07 - Screw plywood

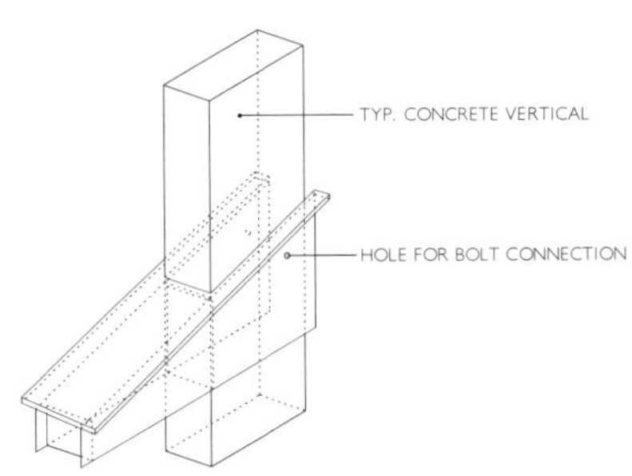

Step 08 - Attach to vertical

11_ Details of proposed plywood formwork for in-situ casting of fins

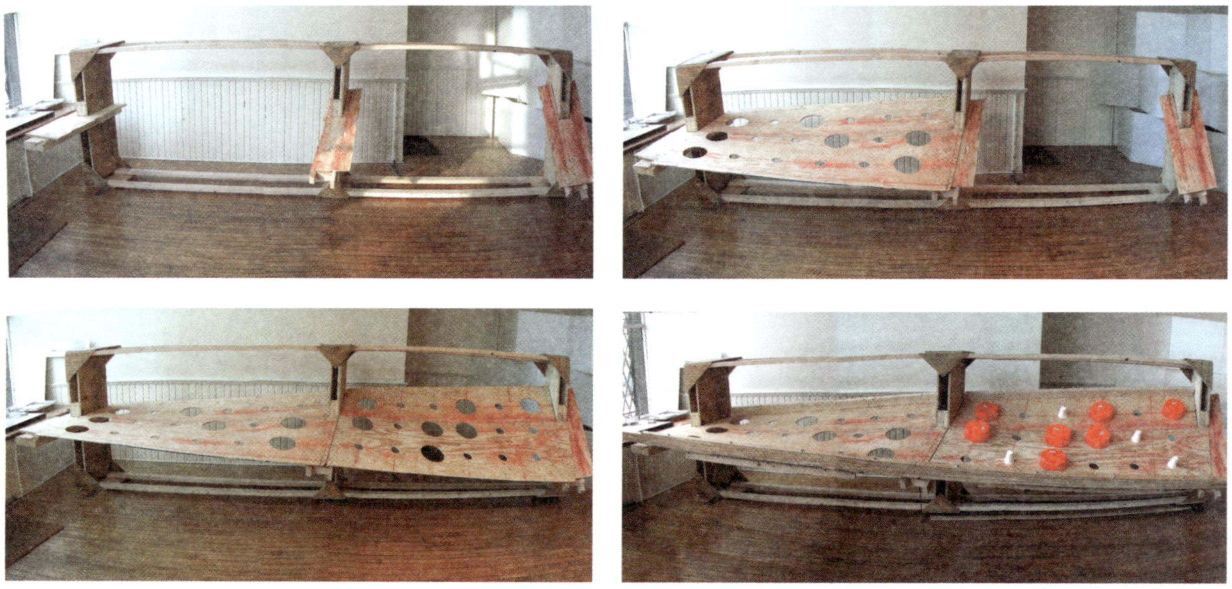

12_ Fin construction images and diagrams from Buffalo office

13_ The pre-cast fin solution

for all forty fins vertically. Each fin, in our proposal, would be cast in place, using a plywood formwork. Once stripped, the formwork would be moved up to the next fin, reconfigured to the correct angles, as it was designed to do, and the next concrete fin would be cast. We forwarded our experiments to our counterparts in Shantou. **(Figure 11, page 111 and Figure 12, opposite page)**

Soon thereafter, our partners in China came back to us with a steel mold solution, built like a table, with potential of adjustment at all four legs. This single mold was able to produce all possible fin configurations. In their proposal, the fins would not be cast as a continuous element wrapping the East, South and West faces of the building. Rather, they would be cast in pieces, a total of fifty-five pieces per fin layer, and then hung on the vertical elements. The efficiency proposed by this system was many times higher than our initial plywood mold, cast-in-place, proposal. However, this proposal left a gap, physically, between each pair of pre-cast fins to be addressed on site. To add to the complexity, our initial system of casting in place had resolved the problem of transition between curves by virtue of a calculated slide between layers of the tested plywood, permitting a seamless and smooth transition at each vertical member. In essence two imaginary fin segments would meet along a perfect surface, both fins maintaining a ninety-degree angle to the formwork and meeting perfectly along that surface at the point of transition. In the pre-cast solution, the ends of each fin would be at ninety degrees to the cast surface as well. Because the transition from curve to curve could not be accommodated within a single mold, the two mating surfaces of a pair of fins would not have exactly the same angle and thus would leave an infinitesimal wedge-shaped gap. This gap is conceptually a part of the problem of the pre-cast system that remained unresolved, a gap between the imagined and the constructed. Despite our attempts to provide a transition solution to the pre-cast system, each solution drew the pre-cast system away from its mass-production capabilities, and enforced a crafted solution. The gap remained in the system and is visible on the building, as constructed. **(Figure 13, opposite page)**

In the same way that the fins on the building façade modulated many functional and aesthetic roles, by deciding to construct the landscape with the same fins, we were able to layer additional modulation roles. The entry landscape incorporates two sets of stairs, an accessible surface, skylights for the basement, parking, as well as designated areas for different types of plants and water features. The ability of the fins to modulate different angles meant that, once properly aligned, they could produce an accessible surface. Yet at the same time, with a slight rotation, they could serve as stairs. Once twisted to a vertical condition, they could easily serve as troughs holding earth or water to support landscape features. The same troughs, could also serve as day-lighting elements. In effect, we were able to propose a horizontal continuation of the façade fins and produce a highly modulated landscape from it.

Our landscaping proposal took shape from ideas that we developed for the north façade. In the same way that we layered the nine different glazing types with three different glazing depths (flush, reversed, recessed) to produce twenty seven variations, we layered the four fin angles with six vertical landscaping dimensions in order to produce twenty four garden types. We proposed water, agate stone, grass, flowers, shrubs, and bamboo, all of indigenous type, each with a particular growth height to satisfy particular landscaping aims and responsibilities. For example, on the north side immediately adjacent to the building, we could only use surfaces and planting that would not prohibit a fire truck from entering the site in case of fire, hence no bamboo or shrubs in that zone. Once again, we were able to propose a crafted composition from a limited set of variables. In this case, of course, all of the systems would have been overlaid with the natural variations of vegetation. The landscaping proposal, unfortunately, was not constructed, creating yet another gap between the imagined and the constructed. **(Figures 14-15, pages 114-115)**

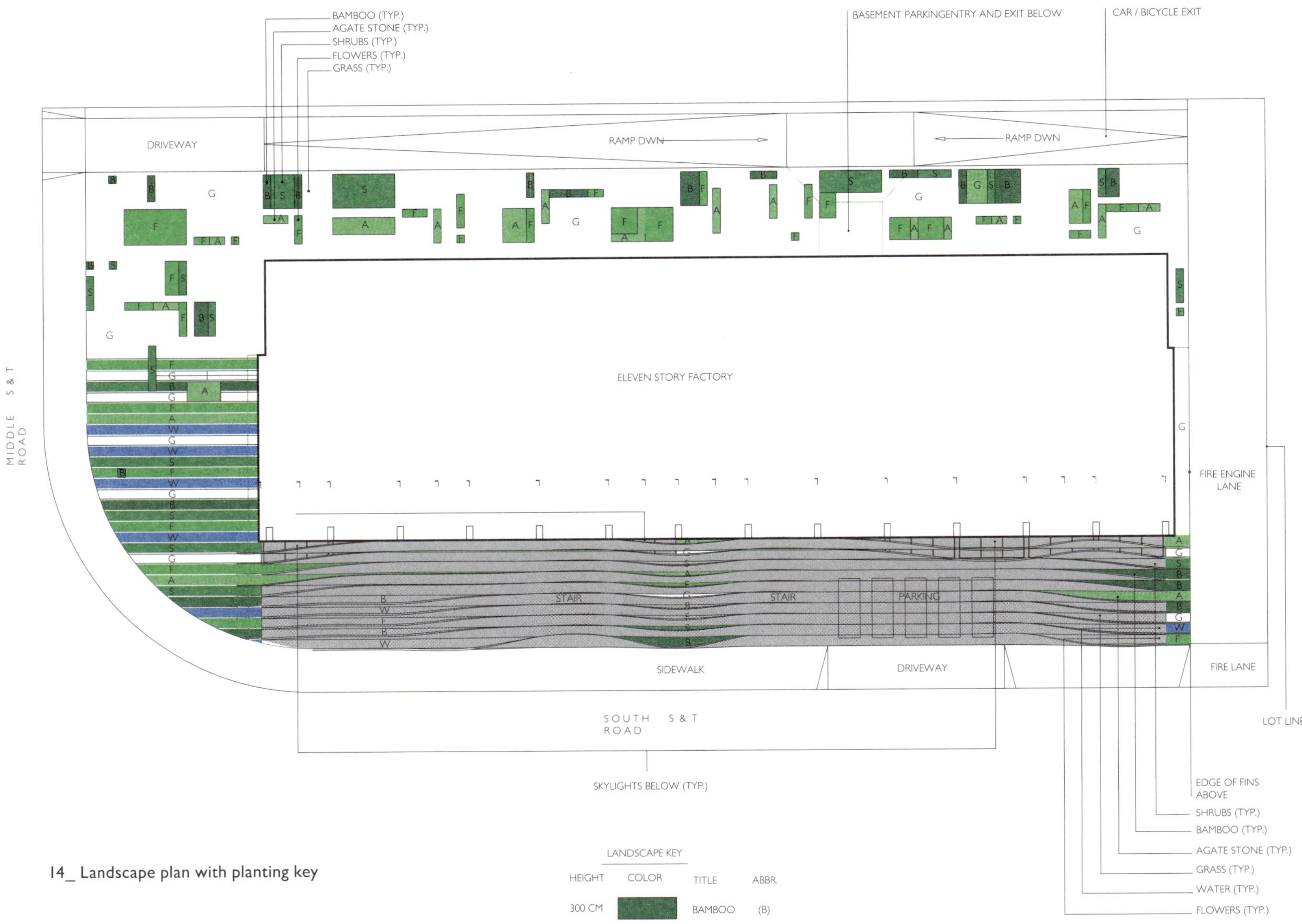

14_ Landscape plan with planting key

LANDSCAPE KEY

HEIGHT	COLOR	TITLE	ABBR
300 CM		BAMBOO	(B)
90 CM		SHRUBS	(S)
45 CM		FLOWERS	(F)
10 CM		GRASS	(G)
5 CM		AGATE STONE	(A)
0 CM		WATER	(W)

15_ Model images of landscape studies

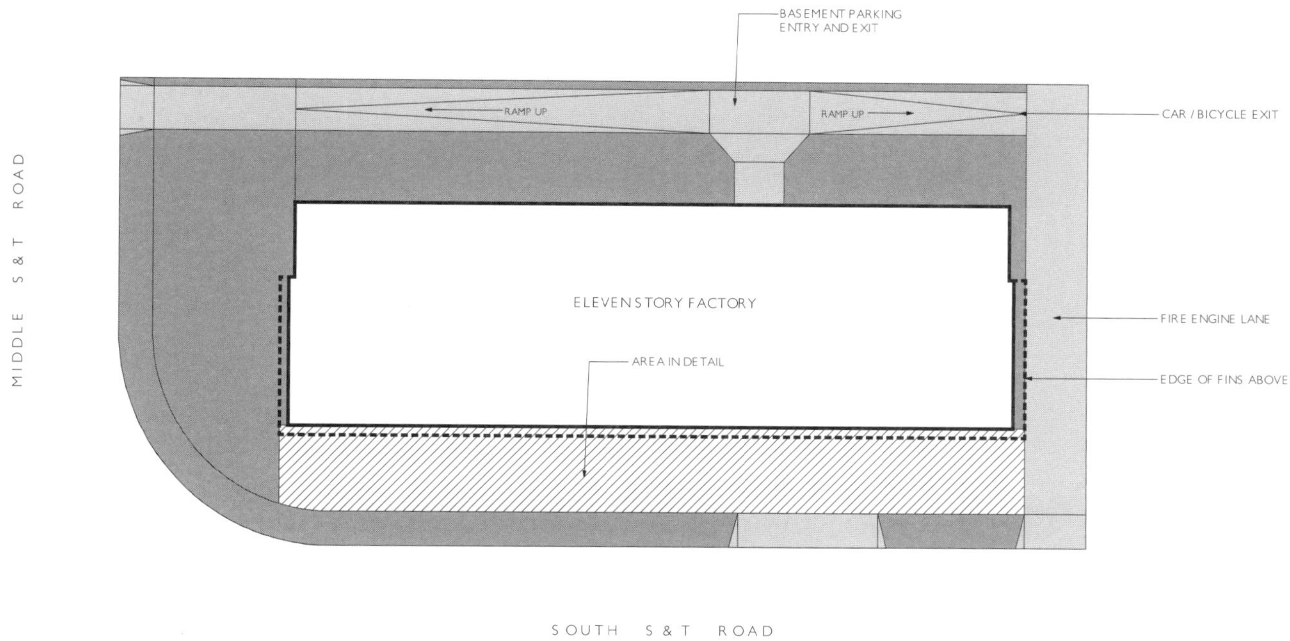

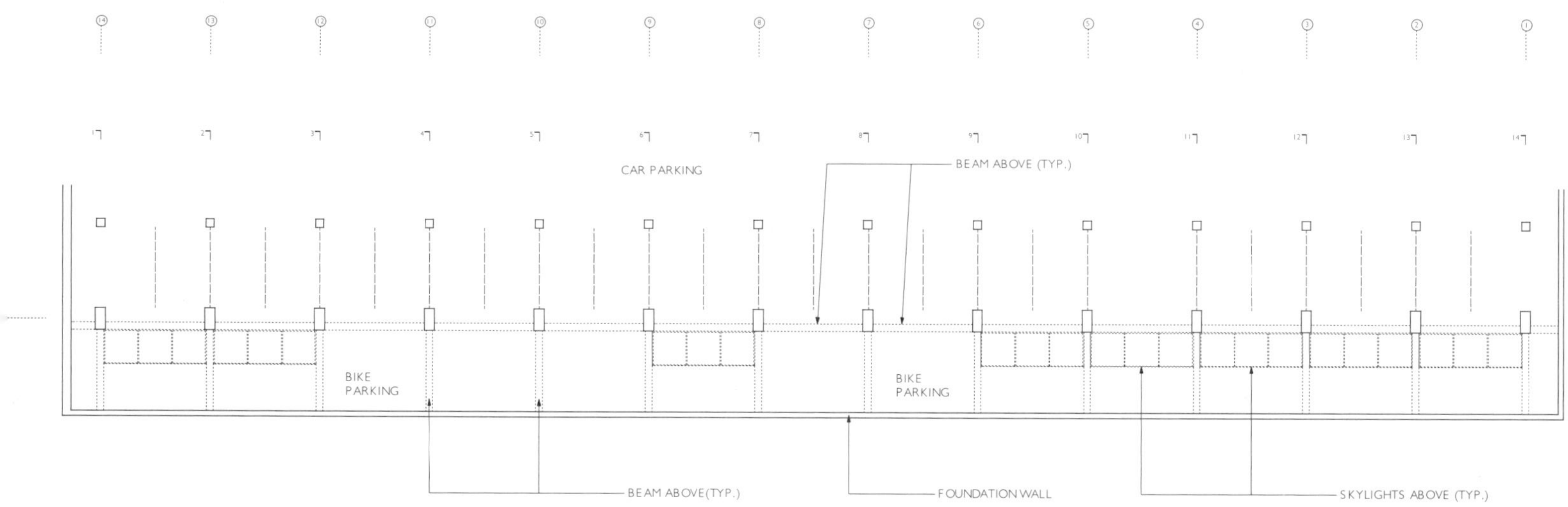

16_ Basement plan describing skylights

Interlude
Tsz Yan Ng

Concrete Twist on Labor

Anyone that has designed and built internationally can attest to the difficulty of negotiating a broad range of challenges in realizing a building. An obvious one being the language differences which a translator could manage. Time differences as well, which sometimes serve to everyone's advantage in getting quick responses where the end of day at one end is the beginning of another. The many challenges between designing a building as imagined and realizing it outside the domain of one's familiarity are themselves a project. L-148 is no exception. The challenges that emerged were perhaps not that different than any architectural work built in a foreign context. The project was to design an efficient garment factory with other programmatic entities that would be pleasant in which to work. More aspirationally, the building would express the essence of the label Lafayette 148 New York – of modern clothing designs, crafted with the highest quality in direct contrast to fast fashion. This seemed direct enough. The additional challenge, or rather something that we sought to understand and embrace, had to do with the reality of building in China, with its unique practices driven largely by regional customs and issues of labor – of people, skills, and means of production. The following reflection highlights aspects of our experience in realizing a building in China, navigating through a complex set of circumstances that not only inform and shape our design decisions but also direct our understanding of our labor as designers in contemporary architectural practice.

Concrete China

In China the on-site construction tradition and low-cost labor market have married and given birth to an unseen quantity of built masses and an unprecedented speed of urban growth. Concrete plays a major role in this state of China. Everyone hears that anything that can be designed can be built, but every architect voices frustration at the lack of training and rigor in construction labor and materials, which are imperative in achieving the highest architectural quality. Concrete lies at the origin of this frustration. Concrete has offered speed, it has offered jobs, and it has created China's current growth pattern. If one were to graph two lines representing cement production per capita and the national's gross domestic product per capita, they would run perfectly parallel.[1]
Qingyun Ma

Concrete historically has been developed with two separate types of labor. The labor of casting in concrete, as Adrian Forty has described, is split between unskilled labor (that of manual work following prescribed instructions on-site) and intellectual labor (that which resides in specialized concrete engineering and designs for formwork and mixes). The split between unskilled and intellectual labor developed, according to Forty, synchronously with specialization in building practices and engineering. Other concurrent developments include the relationship between levels and availability of craft, the confluence of technological shifts, advancements in industrial methodologies, and geopolitical contingencies.[2] For concrete architecture, this split is ever-present today. We see low skill migrant workers in China, moving from rural areas to urban centers as construction jobs are more readily available. In other parts of the world such as Abu Dhabi, workers are even imported to build complex projects by star architects. As a discipline, how do we then measure or demonstrate concretely the different forms of labor of all those who participated from conception to inhabitation? How could labor negotiate design when the building industry is already steeped with protocols and specialized roles? What is then the labor in contemporary architectural practice and discourse, besides the labor it takes to navigate such a complicated system? Only to be complicit to find oneself resigned to designing with accepted industry standards that, as some already intimated, could even be computationally scripted for direct output and optimized for maximum efficiency? Since concrete is so ubiquitously used around the world, building in concrete - its methods and standards of construction - may shed light on this matter.

Formwork making to cast concrete is one of the most labor-intensive processes for building and is often the largest portion of projects' overall cost. While prefabrication has made the use of concrete more cost-effective and time-efficient, poured-in-place concrete is still labor intensive. For typical concrete construction in China, the question of labor is more about manual work than it is about quality or skills. Most construction is covered by a finished coat and, as a result, the original pour need not be precise. Even the concrete mix is generally poor quality. With most rigid reinforced frame structures out of concrete, members are generally oversized to account for inferior mixes. Refined casting, along with better grades of mixes, are usually reserved for public infrastructural work where the concrete is exposed as a finished surface and better structural performance is expected.

Our initial impression with the concrete construction in Shantou, China, was that the quality was not the best. A city whose industry mostly consists of light manufacturing, from clothing to toys, Shantou is not a place where architectural aesthetics, much less concrete architecture, was of utmost importance. Concrete was, and still is, a material for practical building, ranging in types from commercial to housing. With Shantou's seismic concerns, almost all buildings are constructed with poured-in-place rigid reinforced concrete frames with brick infill for walls. All surfaces are then either plastered over with cement or tiled. Because we intended to have the concrete surfaces exposed for our design, our client hired a concrete specialist to oversee the quality as well as an external inspector who ensure there was no substandard use that would compromise the building's structural integrity.[3]

In Shantou, all formwork for concrete casting is produced manually because labor is cheap and abundant. One of our earlier discussions with the builders in Shantou, with typical factory building systems in mind, was if prefabricated T-slabs were available. Their response was that they do not have any precasting in the region. It seemed at first odd given that prefabricated reinforced concrete building systems have been around for well over a century. Particularly those developed for factories, such as those by the Kahn Brothers' marketed as Truscon and later Kahncrete. On second thought, it made a lot of sense. Prefabrication is mainly developed and used for situations where labor is in short supply and buildings need to go up quickly. Since labor is cheap and always available, there is literally no need to develop such systems. Speed however is key to China's burgeoning urban development. But ultimately, with a population of over 1.3 billion people, the labor force could easily make up for speed.[4] In the case of L-148, labor was certainly available, but there was still a limit as to how much work a single construction crew could accomplish on site each day. This was remedied by having both a day and night shift for construction, completing approximately one floor per month. While other metropolitan cities like Beijing and Shanghai can boast more astounding construction rates, the work at Shantou was a speedy endeavor, considering that everything was cast on site.

Concrete Twist

While prefabrication was not available in the region, the concepts and logic of precast system were very much present for L-148. As mentioned in Modulating (**Pages 105-117**), the twisted brise-soleil textile-like façade system, originally developed with a cast-in-place process, was shifted to a precast system. This was due to two interrelated factors: first, the introduction of reusable steel molds for casting, and secondly, in translating the twisting fins into an assembly system of family of parts, the number of angles at the vertical connection needed to be limited and the logic of the system be communicated through diagrams and drawings with our partner firm in China. **(Figure 8, page 108)** Our final design utilizes a total of five different reference angles (0°, 18°, 36°, 54°, and 72°) configured in combinations to create a smooth continuous twist. Only a total of eight types of adjustable steel formworks were necessary for the entire brise-soleil façade layer, accounting for corner and end conditions. The precast system also ensured a consistent level of craft that is not always guaranteed with concrete work in China.

The challenge of developing non-rectilinear formwork for casting was intentional on two levels. It was for us, not only to invent the techniques for realizing the textile-like façade that wraps the building volume and modulates the various environmental concerns, but also to make sure our partner firm in China would continue to work with us during construction and ensure a continuous collaborative relationship for the duration of the project. Too often, design teams in the US and Europe who build in China, hand off a project sketch during schematic design, only to have their service no longer needed once the image of the building is created. That image guides the final exterior look of the building with little regard for material performance, corresponding details, interior organization of program and services, or spatial experience. Without being cynical in this regard, we wanted to by-pass this concern and focus on the real labor of the project, which was to engage critically in the myriad design and construction challenges along every phase of the project.

We were fortunate to have our partner firm, the Shantou City Construction Consortium, to take a giant leap with us in developing, testing, and realizing the façade system and other building components for L-148. The use of post-tensioning for the building's main structure was the first in the region. The choice enabled us to not only span much further without column interruptions for the factory floor, but also to maintain thinner ratios between the structure and the overall volume in which sizing for columns and beams are typically much more robust. The use of post-tensioning not only shifted the engineering and building process that our partners were used to, but also, and maybe more importantly, the use of concrete in this manner shifted their conception of how concrete could perform. It was now possible that concrete could be thin and stable, and be appropriate for a manufacturing facility. Between the use of post-tensioning and the research and development for an unusual process for forming the twisted fins, the labor of our collaboration beyond realizing something wholly new and unique in concrete was to critically re-conceptualize, or twist, the standards for how concrete was imagined and shaped in this region.

Concrete Factory

The process of building in concrete is, in a sense, a prescribed form of manufacturing. There is an order to production, each step measurable in terms of time and types of labor. In fact, concrete construction, as first developed for the building industry, was framed in the same vein as factory production. The development of concrete building systems in the nineteenth century coincided with scientific management of workers' labor to optimize efficiency. Pioneered by Frederick Taylor, Taylorism was the study of factory production in which every task performed by workers was analyzed to reach maximum efficiency, leading to more profitable outputs. Six years before his most famous text, *Principles of Scientific Management* (1911), Taylor along with a concrete engineer Sanford Thompson published *Treatise on Concrete* (1905). In it, every single task involved in constructing something out of concrete is broken down and calculated with the amount of time necessary to complete each task. The goal was to provide a reliable means to calculate the cost of building in concrete. Unsatisfied with the first book's estimation, they produced with even greater details a second book, *Concrete Costs* (1912).[5]

An even more direct link between scientific management and concrete construction is Frank Gilbreth, famous for his stop-motion photography to study movement of workers to optimize productivity. Before embarking on scientific management, Gilbreth was a successful contractor from the east coast of the United States, with a number of large buildings, such as offices and power stations, built in concrete. His obsession with organizational management for building led him to produce a set of standard operating instructions for his employees called *Field System* and later followed by *Concrete System* in 1908 which identified specifically his methods for building in concrete.[6] Such measured forms of labor, highlight the close proximity by which labor is conceived relative to concrete casting and factory production. In each, labor and time is quantifiable and cost is predictable. For both Taylor and Gilbreth, modeling the process of concrete casting the same way a factory might function was motivated by the desire to reach maximum efficiency and, therefore, profitability. This is possible with the assumption that all the laborers are similarly skilled or, in the case of concrete, could be unskilled unlike other forms of building trades such as carpentry or metal work.

For L-148, the process for casting the twisted panels, as a system, parallels a factory's production logic. Once construction of a single floor was completed, the factory floor was set up with steel molds as the site to precast the façade panels. In this sense, the first thing that the building produced was in fact itself. Each panel measures 7ft x 3 ¼ ft x 8 inches thick (216.67cm x 100cm x 20cm) and weighs over 600 lbs. The panels cast on one floor, were not for the same floor but for the floor below so that when it was time to install, the panels were lowered into place rather than hoisted upward. This level of efficiency, in the process of managing the casting and installation of 2,440 panels, was in itself reflective of industrial factory production. While the manufacturing of these panels as a system is a form of prescribed process – with the construction logic grounded in combinatory design and prefabrication – the panel design developed through prototyping, emphasized both the intellectual and manual labor involved in its production. The spatial and organizational logic during construction no doubt has its roots in labor optimization for manufacturing.

Concrete Labor

Beyond the close affinities that clothing and architecture as allied disciplines share, the experience afforded through working on L-148 points to an interesting parallel between contemporary architecture and the garment industry, namely that they are both considered to be global manufacturing industries. In this sense, these industries have followed trajectories guided by technology, material innovation, economic forces, and geopolitical influences. Sourcing, transportation, labor, import/export duties, and numerous other factors determine the making of manufactured goods and such influences are often extremely complex to follow.[7] It is often hard to keep track, for instance, of the smaller segment of outsourced production. It is often difficult to know, for example, the origin of one component part in relation to the finished whole. For clothing manufacturing, the product is much smaller compared to architecture and much more mobile. The manufacture of clothing's rate of change is seasonal and, in the case of China, what is shown on catwalks one day can be duplicated the next. The tools and associated techniques for manufacturing are nimbler as compared to architecture. As such, the general pace of cyclical change is a lot faster. Aside from the obvious difference that architecture presents, being more demanding in terms of scale and resources to produce, architecture as a building industry is steeped in protocols and traditions. Life safety concerns alone account for decades upon decades of adjustments in regulations. Material systems for buildings are specialized and engineered, requiring extensive testing, making innovations incremental. As a result, architecture as an industry is slow to change. Known and tried systems are used repeatedly as any single architectural firm does not have the resources or the qualified knowledge to simply invent new modes of production. While these factors do not necessarily make the building industry global (though sourcing alone probably confirms that it is, even at the scale of a house), architecture, or practice today is not geographically bound. An architectural firm can have projects being built in Europe, Asia, or Africa, employing the same material and techniques for building. A particular curtain-wall system in the US can be the same in China. If a certain material is not available, it can be shipped. In fact, for corporate firms that have projects around the world, drawing details are ready and available at the click of a button. Global, in this sense, is similar to clothing and may imply speed and efficiency, but it may also promote sameness just as quickly.

At the core of global manufacturing is labor. Both the garment and the building industry rely on cheap manual labor as the basis for its production. Low-skilled labor is universally applicable. The same skills needed to sew a shirt in Bangladesh are the same skills necessary in China. The same goes for construction (especially in relation to concrete casting processes) where methods of building could be imported as needed. We see similar grievances for the treatment of workers in both industries. And, given architecture's scale of production, migrant workers often remain not only within their native country as garment workers do, but are imported to foreign places where labor might be scarce or the type of work is undesirable for citizens of that nation.[8] For the garment industry, outsourcing to developing countries, takes advantage of cheap labor for a wider profit margin when goods are exported from the place of production. For architecture, migrant workers gravitate toward places where building activities are concentrated. Between the movement of people, things, and their activities, labor, in the global context for both industries is difficult to grasp, and even harder to represent. While manufacturing industries are dependent and in large part defined by it, labor is largely invisible, especially in the final product.

Similar to the garment industry, there is currently a lot of attention in the media and from socially motivated activists about the mistreatment of migrant workers for the building industry. While this makes visible the laborers, and is a good reminder even for architects that we participate in a manufacturing industry with social and ethical implications, it often falls under the mechanism of exposé reporting. What L-148 offers, is an alternative way to potentially and effectively work with labor. In the project, the aesthetics and ethos of building, through the construction logic and crafting, is in fact the formal expression of the design. This shifts the attention away from the need to represent the intrinsic act of labor as in doing the labor (as in the images of factory workers toiling in horrid conditions from nineteenth century Europe or twenty-first century Asia), or some reliance on the necessity of the material artifact to read or embody labor (as in the inordinate admiration bestowed on an object regardless of functional or aesthetic value simply by virtue of having been handcrafted). For L-148, our work was not to perpetuate the rhetoric of these images to call attention to these aspects of labor. While we did have garment workers in mind in the design of this building and handcrafting is part of the casting process for the concrete, labor for us was not something scrutinized outside of design and building. Labor was enacted as an intrinsic and vital part of the design and building.

While labor is key in the discussion of L-148, the project also sponsored to highlight two aspects of labor in contemporary architectural practice today that is not exclusive to building in concrete or in China. The first issue is the separation of craft between the intellectual (architect as designer) to that of the manual (labor of the builder). This separation highlights the fact that architects are moving away from the tradition of master builders – where the architects have the command of how to build as much as the builders. This shift has to do with technical specializations such as acoustics, lighting, HVAC, and sustainable solutions, all consultation services that encompass a large portion of design practice today. It is more difficult for architects to literally master the comprehensive nature of designing a building in its entirety. Additionally, certain global practices value building methodologies that are known and tested over those that might be more experimental. Higher construction cost and completion delays usually prevent designers from going outside of prescriptive norms.

The second aspect, implicit in the reconsideration of crafting or perhaps in response to, proposes design innovation to be a form of heuristic knowledge – what constitutes design research for the building industry as a model of collaborative exchange between builder/specialists and designers.[9] In this regard, prototyping is key. Rather than designers specifying to the builder a process for building that is predetermined, prototyping and testing are necessary to inform the design and production. In this regard, architects work with the builders early on to identify challenges and implement solutions. This sense of crafting not only considers the techniques for building in terms of materiality and processes, but also identifies crafting as a process, a methodology for making, testing, drawing, and remaking. Renzo Piano aptly describes this process:

An architect must be a craftsman. Of course, any tools will do. These days the tools might include a computer, an experimental model and mathematics. However, it is still craftsmanship – the work of someone who does not separate the work of the mind from the work of the hand. It involves a circular process that draws you from an idea to a drawing, from a drawing to an experiment, and from a construction back to an idea again. For me this cycle is fundamental to creative work.[10]

Rather than lamenting on the separation between architect and builder, this sense of crafting is perhaps more productive given how contemporary practice is leaning. In this context, crafting recalibrates the role of each player, and challenges each in terms of expertise outside of normative praxis. For L-148, the building along with the twisted fins, was not just concepts drawn and represented, handed to the builder. Our design was critically informed by the recursive process of production. The overall design did not rely on a predetermined existing construction system, but rather sought to develop the system with the labor available and the capabilities of the local building trade. The formwork for the twisted fins especially, can be considered as the site of labor and as a product of creative exchange. There were parameters to consider as well as limitations, even concessions between how we originally imagined certain details to be and how it ultimately was built. Rather than focusing on the inconsistent gaps between what we as designers had in mind versus how they the builder might have failed to meet our expectation, the relay of exchanges that shaped and gave expression to L-148 was what enabled the project to evolve. Ultimately our role as designers was to recognize that these series of exchanges and responses, our labor, were critical to not only realizing L-148 but also in how we engage contemporary practice.

Concrete Image

Since the completion of the building in 2009, there are many built works around the world that highlight concepts present in L-148. These include digital fabrication of mass-produced building component manufacturing with the logic of prefabrication of family of parts. Also, with CNC technologies, experiments in non-rectilinear concrete forming are prevalent. At first glance, L-148 has often been mistaken as a parametrically driven design. Certainly, concepts of combinatory compositional logic and twisting concrete forms, responding to various design and construction parameters are present. However, the façade was not algorithmically derived. Additionally, some may bill L-148 as a sustainable project since the double-layered façade system and passive cooling techniques together managed climate control without sole reliance on mechanical systems. However, we did not design L-148 to advance the agendas of sustainable green architecture. L-148 was not designed to fit neatly in any singular category of contemporary architectural discourse, nor does it present or prioritize the image of one type of architecture over another. The brise-soleil concrete façade layer is not an independent mask for an inner hermetically sealed building where the façade could be replaced with any other design. It is literally wedded with the rest of the building, spatially, environmentally, and experientially. Ultimately, this project was not about creating a container with which to fill any programs. It was conceived predominantly as a factory to respond to what actually takes place inside – garment factory work and the various types of labor that necessitate human crafting.

The L-148 building as it stands today seems composed, as if everything is in its logical place. Outside, a flowing textile-like façade wraps around the building. Inside, workers perform their tasks in a bright, clean, and comfortable environment. Not a drop of sweat is in sight. This is not the image we normally associate with in regard to garment manufacturing facilities, especially in China.

L-148 is the result of a confluence of factors that emerged in a specific moment in time. The garment industry in New York since the 1990s was already starting to outsource to countries with cheaper labor than that found in New York. Lafayette 148 New York is one of the many companies that had to follow suit to stay competitive. They did not adopt the model of fast fashion, however, but saw garment manufacturing as vertically integrated in order to have more control over design and quality. The driving force of L-148, the CEO of the company Mr. Sun Yut Siu, had a vision of not only what it takes for Lafayette 148 to thrive as a fashion label in the global economy but also in what Lafayette 148 sponsors in terms of jobs and opportunities for the people of Shantou – as a form of paying forward the grace he received there as an orphan child. Even the site for this building, a newly developed area for industries in the city when we started in 2005, is now fully integrated into the dense urban fabric. Land speculation today would have made this project too costly. The construction frenzy was at an all-time high. Shantou, while less prominent than the city of Shenzhen as the face of China's manufacturing boom, or Shanghai and Beijing as the image of its rise to global economic power, is a city that still had room for experimentation. Its steady growth did not choke the building industry to conform to developer precepts or replicate a standard image of modernization. Shantou, as a city, escaped this fate. If any of those circumstances were different, it would have meant a very different design for L-148.

Clearly, there were parameters to work with and Qingyun Ma was correct to say that in China, anything designed could be built – however frustrated with craftsmanship one might be. But as we know, the image of a design might be quite different than what it actually becomes when built. Perhaps because of the lack of imaging in Shantou or a place where building as a craft can still be explored, other images could emerge; a garment factory where workers are at ease, a building in the urban environment that breaths, a textile-like façade that modulates a building's interior comfort, a concrete façade that dematerializes by something as ephemeral as light. **(Figure 1-2, pages 126-127)** All these images are made possible by the fact that there was the space for experimentation and L-148, not just a factory, but as a device for thinking, continues to generate new images for us to reflect upon. We are fortunate and grateful not only for the building to perform the way it does programmatically and actually but also continues to do so imaginatively.

Endnotes

1 Ma, Qingyun. "The State of Concrete: An Investigation of Concrete in China," in *Solid States, Concrete in Transition*, ed. by Michael Bell and Craig Buckley. New York: Princeton Architectural Press. 2010, p. 218.

2 See Forty, Adrian. *Concrete and Culture, A Material History.* London: Reaktion Books Ltd, 2013, 14-22, 225-235.

3 Rampant in different regions of China are poorly built work due to use of substandard quality material. Recall the Wenchuan quake of 2008 in Sichuan province where schools constructed by public authorities collapsed more readily than other buildings.

4 Population estimate at the time when the L148 was completed. For an example of how labor dictates prefabrication research and develop, see Forty p.116 on Frankfurt's social housing situation in the early part of the 20th C.

5 For a detailed account of concrete and scientific management, see Forty, 236-239. Also ref., F.W. Taylor, *Principles of Scientific Management.* New York: Harper & Brothers, 1911. F.W. Taylor and Sanford E. Thompson, *A Treatise on Concrete Plain and Reinforced, Materials Construction, and Design of Concrete and Reinforced Concrete,* 3rd ed. New York: John Wiley & Sons, 1905. F.W. Taylor and Sanford E. Thompson, *Concrete Costs; Tables and Recommendations for Estimating the Time and Cost of Labor Operations in Concrete Construction and for Introducing Economical Methods of Management.* New York: Wiley & Sons, 1912.

6 See Forty, 236-239, Frank B. Gilbreth, *Field System.* New York: M.C. Clark Publishing Co., 1908, pp. 113-118, and *Concrete System.* New York: The Engineering News Publishing Co., 1908. For Taylor's contribution on factory designs in the early part of the 20th Century, see Carter's essay, p. 36-37.

7 There are many studies by economists tracing the global production of clothing manufacturing, particularly the life cycles of clothing as it relates to consumer habits and environmental impact. For a good reference, see Pietra Rivoli's *The Travels of a T-Shirt in the Global Economy: An Economist Examines the Markets, Power, and Politics of World Trade.* New Jersey: John Wiley & Sons, 2009. For architecture, global building practices are generally discussed in relations to environmental and sustainable practices in term of material sourcing or energy consumption.

8 An exception to this is the case of Chinese garment laborers seeking work in Prato, Italy (as opposed to already transplanted foreign nationals who will take on low-wage labor from different sectors of the economy). For the case of Prato, it is so that the clothing manufactured there could include a 'Made in Italy' label, raising the value of the garment when exported by virtue of association that Italian made goods are of higher quality.

9 For elaboration of various forms of labor in relation to practice and technological shifts, see Peggy Deamer and Phillip G. Bernstein's *Building (in) the Future, Recasting Labor in Architecture.* New York: Princeton Architectural Press, 2010.

10 From Kenneth Frampton's essay "Intention, Craft, and Rationality," in Deamer and Bernstein, p. 34.

ICBC

ICBC
中国工商银行

Project Credits

Project Architect
Mehrdad Hadighi, Principal, Studio for Architecture
in collaboration with Tsz Yan Ng

Design Team
Mehrdad Hadighi, Tsz Yan Ng, Christopher Romano

Architect of Record
Shantou City Construction Consortium

Project Team
Adesh Michael Singh
Michael O'Hara
Jose Chang
Maciej Kaczynski
Dave Nardozzi

Photographic credits

But-Sou Lai Photography
Pages: 2-3, 13, 14-15,20-21, 28-29, 38-39, 50-51, 57-60, 62-63, 72-73, 86-87, 94-95, 102-103, 116-117, 125, 126-127

Mehrdad Hadighi
Pages 105, 112 and collages of page 85

Tsz Yan Ng
Pages: 19, 70-71

Cody Goddard Photography
Page 20, Figures 10-13

Alamy
Page 37

Nina Rappaport
Pages 58, 59

Twisted Image: This is the New Brutal – Mark Linder
Figure 1 – RIBA18327, Figure 2 – Smithson Family Foundation, London, Figure 3 – ma7219 Tate, Figure 4 – Pompidou Inventory number: AM 1993-1-698, Figure 5 – Reyner Banham, *The New Brutalism: Ethic or Aesthetic?*, The Architectural Press, London, 1966, 68., Figure 7 – Henderson Estate, Figure 8 – Pompidou, Figure 9 – M01124 Tate, Figure 10 – German Pavilion, International Exposition, Barcelona, Spain, Interior perspective. 1928-1929. MoMA Mies van der Rohe Archive. © 2013 Artists Rights Society (ARS), New York , Figure 11 – RIchard Hamilton, "Structure," 1950 Etching and aquatint on paper, 400 x 303 mm. c Estate of Richard Hamilton, Tate Images. Figure 12 – Nigel Henderon, Photograph, Hunstanton Secondary School under construction, c. 1953, c.Nigel Henderson Estate, Tate Images, Figure 13 – John Malby, Photograph, 1938. Boots Drys building, John Maltby/RIBA Collections, Figure 14 – Dell and Wainwright, Photograph, 1935. Pioneer Helath Center, Peckham, Architectural Press Archive/ RIBA Collections, Figures 15,16 – Collage by author

Book credits

Published by
Actar Publishers, New York, Barcelona

Editors
Mehrdad Hadighi, Marc J Neveu,
Tsz Yan Ng

Contributors
Brian Carter
Mark Linder
Nina Rappaport

Graphic Design and Digital Production
Papersdoc SL

ISBN: 978-19-40291-94-9
PCN: 2016948657
A CIP catalogue record for this book
is available from Library of Congress,
Washington, D.C., USA

Distribution
Actar D, Inc.

New York
440 Park Avenue South, 17th FL,
NY, NY 10016 US
T +1 212 966 2207
salesnewyork@actar-d.com

Barcelona
Roca i Batlle 2
08023 Barcelona, SP
+34 933 282 183
eurosales@actar-d.com